A Tavola!

GIANNI SCAPPIN AND VINCENZO LAURIA
THE CULINARY INSTITUTE OF AMERICA

Photography by Ben Fink

RECIPES AND REFLECTIONS ON
TRADITIONAL ITALIAN HOME COOKING

LEBHAR-FRIEDMAN BOOKS
NEW YORK • CHICAGO • LOS ANGELES • LONDON • PARIS • TOKYO

PAGES IV AND V, LEFT TO RIGHT: Pasta con Cozze e Fagioli, page 118, Polipo Affogato con Patate Gialle, page 135, Agnello in Umido Profumato alla Menta, page 140; PAGE VI AND OVERLEAF: Peperonata Povera e Pigra, page 153; PAGE VII, LEFT TO RIGHT: Fagioli al Fiasco "Rivisitati," page 149, Fritto Misto, page 150; OPPOSITE: Peposo di Manzo con la Zucca, page 144

Images on pages iv–v, xii–xv, xvii, 4–5, 35, 57, 60–61, 73, 83–85, 95, 100, 121, 124–125, 133, 162–163, 168, 177, 187, and 191 appear courtesy of the Library of Congress; images on pages ii–iii, vi–vii, 1, 79–81, 157 © Photodisc, Inc.; images on pages xix, 122–123, 158–159 © Kevin Hanek; image on pages 2–3 appears courtesy of the authors.

LIBRARY OF CONGRESS CATALOGING-IN-PUBLICATION DATA

Cataloging-in-publication data for this title is on file with the Library of Congress.

ISBN 978-0-86730-928-7

THE CULINARY INSTITUTE OF AMERICA

President: Dr. Tim Ryan

Vice-President, Dean of Culinary Education: Mark Erickson

Director of Publishing: Nathalie Fischer

Editorial Project Manager: Mary Donovan

Recipe Testing Manager: Maggie Wheeler

LEBHAR-FRIEDMAN BOOKS

A company of Lebhar-Friedman, Inc., 425 Park Avenue, New York, New York 10022

Publisher: Maria Tufts

Art Director: Kevin Hanek

Manufactured in Malaysia on acid-free paper

TABLE OF CONTENTS

CHAPTER ONE

Antipasti e Zuppe: Small Dishes and Soups 5

THIS BOOK IS a collection of some of our favorite recipes. We come from separate parts of Italy, but share a common love of Italian foods and Italian traditions (even when our traditions differ). Italian life is centered around the family. The table is where the family comes together every day to share great food and wine.

There is never an argument about that, even though Gianni grew up in Marostica, in Italy's Veneto region, and Vincenzo in Napoli (Naples). Sure, we disagree about how much (if any) garlic you should add to the sauce, and a host of other fine points, because, of course, we have our traditions to defend! You are hereby granted dispensation from unearthing the "best" and "most authentic" version of *pesto* or *gnocchi*, however, as long as you promise to approach your kitchen and your table with enthusiasm.

Throughout the book you will find both treasured family recipes and "new" dishes inspired by the great foods we've enjoyed on our travels. We've visited trattorias and pensiones, we've recalled the special dishes our neighbors and family members take such pride in,

and we've experimented with some New World foods handled with an Old World sensibility. We've drawn from our experiences in restaurants in the United States and inserted our memories of our Italian homes. We both have loved ones who still prefer to forage for bitter greens in the field rather than buy them from a market, and pluck the blossoms from their home-grown zucchini plants instead of bringing them home in a little plastic carton. Not everyone is as blessed when it comes to food as the Italians, and not everyone has access to mountain fields or garden plots, but that should never stop you. It seems as if the whole world is jumping on the fresh, local, and seasonal bandwagon. We believe that the Italians are the ones saving seats for the rest of the world.

Turning our recipes and stories into a book was a group effort. We both want to thank Dr. Tim Ryan for his support, Tom Peer for encouraging us to take on the project, and a host of students and teaching assistants, in particular our assistants Tyler, Dylan, Alex, Beth, Angela, and Joseph, and our partners at the restaurant, Chefs Dwayne LiPuma and Alberto Vanoli.

The heart of great Italian dining can be expressed in a few words: simple, fresh, flavorful, and traditional. All Italians agree on simple, fresh, and flavorful: locally harvested fruits and vegetables, seafood fresh from the ocean, finely crafted cheeses and cured meats, lively wines that taste of the sun and the earth, oil pressed from the fruit of ancient olive groves using time-honored techniques. We prefer marketing every day and gathering our large families together on Sundays and holidays. The traditions, of course, are personal; each family is unique. We hope that with this book, you can sample some of our favorite traditions, and perhaps make a few of your own.

This book is dedicated to my mom and dad, whose love of cooking and food inspired me, and to Christian, my son, who has always been very loving and understanding throughout my career. I am grateful that finally we found each other again. And special thanks to my best friend, Lois, whose continuous support and sincere friendship kept me going through the final stages of this project.

— GIANNI SCAPPIN

I dedicate this book to my entire family. I want to express a special gratitude to someone who raised me to appreciate the wonderful world of Italian cuisine—my mother, Nunzia. Finally, I would like to thank Jeff for his immense love, kindness, and support—I am blessed to have you in my life.

— VINCENZO LAURIA

ITALIAN CULINARY TRADITIONS

A BRIEF HISTORY

To FIND THE origins of Italian cooking traditions, we look first to the Magna Grecia (Latin for "greater Greece"), the area of southern Italy and Sicily colonized by Greek settlers, who brought the Hellenistic traditions of the old empire along with them. Their daily meals were simple (pork, salted fish, chickpeas, lentils, olives, pickles, and dried figs) but at banquets the food was more varied and plentiful. The ancient Romans tell of sumptuous feasts held by the Etruscans featuring soups, game in vinegar and honey sauces, and sweets with almonds and walnuts.

For their part, however, the early Romans were a sober, frugal people who took only two meals a day, lunch and supper. By the time we reach the Roman Imperial Age, the custom of a breakfast of cereal, honey, dried fruit, and cheese had been introduced. Dinner was the main meal: a feast of *antipasti* (mixed seafood), followed by game, pork, veal, goat, fowl, and fish, in turn followed by sweet dishes, as well as fresh and dried fruits. These courses were accompanied by sweet, scented wines.

During the Middle Ages, with most of the Italian population reduced to poverty, meals typically consisted of cereals, milk, cheese, and vegetables. After the Crusades, however, with much of Europe starting to recover from the Dark Ages and emerging into the Renaissance, the demand for spices and exotic foodstuffs grew. Since there was a fixed route for the trade, which led directly to the powerful city-states of Italy, notably Venice, it is no great surprise that Italian food was influenced. It was not just spices, of course. Rice, spinach, and peas all arrived from the East along with silks and spices from the Orient.

Attempts to circumvent the traditional route eventually led to exploration of the New World and introduced yet another influx of foods to Italy. Some of these foods, brand new to the country in the sixteenth and seventeenth centuries, are now so firmly established that you may have to think for a minute to remember that tomatoes are a New World food.

Italian cooking reigned supreme throughout Europe from the end of the Middle Ages through the seventeenth century. Catherine de Medici is especially noted for popularizing Italian foods and manners in France: sweets, ice creams, artichokes, broccoli, and tiny peas. Italians were also the original "Ms. Manners" of Europe, and were responsible for what was then a startling innovation: individual cutlery for each person at the table.

In the last several decades, Italian food and cooking has changed as a result of rapid and profound changes in lifestyle. This renowned cuisine is as varied as the terrain—harsh volcanic soil in the South to rich lush mountain areas of the North.

The Regions of Italy

Italy is divided into 20 regions, which are subdivided into a total of 94 provinces. Of the 20 Italian regions, five with special autonomy for ethnic, historical, or peripheral reasons, are:

Valle d'Aosta
Trentino-Alto Adige
Friuli-Venezia Giulia
Sardegna
Sicilia

The remaining 15 regions, with ordinary autonomy, are:

Piemonte
Lombardia
Veneto
Liguria
Emilia-Romagna
Toscana
Umbria
Marche
Lazio
Abruzzo
Molise
Campania
Apulia (Puglia)
Basilicata
Calabria

Each of these regions maintains their own unique culinary traditions, as well as contributing products, cooking techniques, and recipes to the greater fabric of Italian cuisine.

THE CULINARY REGIONS OF ITALY

NORTHERN ITALY

Butter, cream, olive oil, lard, Parmigiano-Reggiano, boiled and braised meats: pork, beef, veal, venison, liver, turkey, speck, prosciutto (San Daniele), mortadella, coppa, freshwater fish and seafood, eel, scampi, salt cod , wheat, corn, rice, beans, risotto and polenta, pasta (ravioli, fettuccine, lasagna, tagliatelle, tortellini, agnolotti. bigoli), gnocchi, apples, pears, cherries, radicchio, cabbage, potatoes, tomatoes, asparagus, beets, onions, peas, porcini mushrooms, white truffles, saffron, caraway, horseradish, paprika, balsamic vinegar

CENTRAL ITALY

Olive oil, lard, herbs, pesto, wine, farinata, sheep's milk cheese, melon, citrus, tomatoes, black cabbage, spinach, fennel, artichokes, peas, chestnuts, walnuts, unsalted bread, white beans, lentils, freshwater fish, seafood, snails, dried cod, fish stews and chowders, black truffles, porcini mushrooms, pepperoncini, pasta (spaghetti, rigatoni, bucatini, egg-based fettuccine, ravioli, maccheroni, spaghetti à la chitarra, papardelle), crêpes, meats (grilled, roasted, fried, spit-roasted): beef, game, lamb, pork, poultry, rabbit

SOUTHERN ITALY

Olive oil, sheep's milk cheese, buffalo mozzarella, citrus, raisins, tomatoes, fennel, potatoes, eggplant, mushrooms, fresh and dried pasta (spaghetti, penne, vermicelli, rigatoni, orechiette), pizza, pepperoncini, sausage, almonds, marzipan, wheat, couscous, beans, oysters, mussels, lamb, goat, pork, venison, wine, saffron, cinnamon, honey, freshwater fish, sardines, anchovies, tuna, swordfish, sweets, chestnuts, hazelnuts, flatbread (carta da musica)

"L'appetito vien mangiando."

Appetite comes while you're eating.

— ITALIAN PROVERB

THE ITALIAN TABLE

THE WORD "GASTRONOMY" has become an important term in the culinary world. It is applied to almost every topic, but when we fail to use this word properly, it loses its meaning and becomes just another trendy catch-phrase.

That doesn't mean we shouldn't use the term. In fact, if we are to talk about Italian cuisine, we must use it. *Gastronomy* has been defined by Brillat-Savarin as "a scientific definition of all that relates to man as a feeding animal. Its object is to watch over the preservation of man by means of the best possible food."

As a nation, and as a collection of distinct culinary regions, Italy has embraced the concept of gastronomy and woven it into the fabric of every meal and even every snack. Because Italians remain intimately attached to their own regions, they have a distinctive tradition of gastronomy to uphold that continues to draw on its ancient foundations.

Italian gastronomy encompasses a significant level of wealth, sophistication, and appreciation for the finer things—things that the Italian people have become masters of down through the centuries. Italians enjoy their slower pace and relish their time spent a tavola (at the table), counting it as one of the finer things of life.

Life unfolds around the Italian table. Italians are famous for being boisterous, flamboyant, dramatic, and theatrical—even loud!—at the table. Do we ever disagree at the table? Well, putting people with different opinions together doesn't always work, but at least gathered around the table we work to create a sense of togetherness, communication, and warmth.

Another important Italian saying, *"a tavola non si invecchia mai"* (you never age at the table) rings true to me. Time spent together around the table strengthens values and reinforces familial customs and traditions. We seem to express ourselves best there. Important decisions, from family matters to politics, are all made at the table, a setting where delicious food and tantalizing beverages are major factors.

Thanks to this tradition, we are a nation of connoisseurs and experts on our gastronomy. We have been blessed and, consequently, have become spoiled by the variety that we expect to enjoy at the table on a daily basis. Italians incorporate gastronomic and religious traditions, as well as customs concerning health and well-being, in dictating what foods should be pre-pared to enjoy on particular days of the week or year. The religious-based tradition of having meat on Thursday, fish on Friday, and soup on Saturday has additional benefits, acting as a sort of natural cleansing to prepare for the Sunday feast and its seeming endless parade of food.

Without doubt daily life in our modern era is very trying. Everything moves at a fast and furious pace. We all aim to meet high standards of achievement. We work insane hours and try to be as productive as we can. Certainly this might result in a form of material happiness. But is this enough? Perhaps for some it is, but for the typical Italian it would never qualify as a completely happy life.

Despite the accelerating pace of daily life, Italians to this day find lunchtime to be their favorite part of the day. Not so long ago, lunch was certainly the main meal of the day. Businesses typically closed for a period of time so lunch could be taken at home with one's family. Dinner was normally served later in the evening and was a lighter meal. Even though more and more Italians face the longer working hours of a more hurried pace of business, and for them, a lunchtime break doesn't allow quite enough time for the luxury of returning home, they still try to recreate both the flavor and the ambience of a home-cooked meal, thanks to the enormous numbers of eateries found all over. There you always find groups of people gathered together eating and engaging in conversation. Contrast that with the typical hurried worker in the United States, often a solitary diner eating in the company of a newspaper.

I have to say, however, that these days more than just goods and products are crossing the Atlantic from the Old World to the New. As visitors cross from one country to another, everyone gains in understanding. Italians are proud that our culture's gastronomic values are an important export, helping everyone to appreciate the importance of taking time to both understand where our food comes from and to enjoy food and wine together at the table. The diet of a typical Italian, today as in the past, includes all the right elements for flavorful, exciting food: healthy ingredients, plenty of vegetables, wine, and a healthy lifestyle we all ought to consider adopting. The quantity and quality of books, television programming, and educational opportunities devoted to teaching young and old alike about the importance of healthy eating and drinking has strengthened this message.

This "slow food" approach is an antidote to the notion that eating in the car or on the go is the same thing as sharing a meal. I see that many people want to know more about this kind of lifestyle. They thirst for great, healthful foods and wines. People are spending more time davanti ai fornelli (in front of the stove) experimenting with new combinations and trying different methods of cooking. The result of all this interest has resulted in greater knowledge about what constitutes great food, more time spent shopping, and greater care in cooking.

ANTIPASTI E ZUPPE

Small Dishes and Soups

CARCIOFINI MARINATI ALL'OLIO D'OLIVA

BABY ARTICHOKES MARINATED IN OLIVE OIL

YOU MAY SIMMER the artichokes in different blends of vinegar and wine. Use more vinegar if you like a very sharp taste. Dilute the mixture with some water for a less intense bite.

SERVES 6

4 cups dry white wine

6 cups white wine vinegar

1 tsp allspice berries

1 tsp kosher salt

4 bay leaves, fresh if available

4 garlic cloves, smashed

24 baby artichokes, cleaned

1 tsp chopped parsley

½ tsp chopped marjoram

4 cups mild olive oil, or as needed

1. Combine the wine, vinegar, allspice berries, salt, bay leaves, and garlic in a large, nonreactive pan (stainless steel or enameled cast iron are best: no aluminum, please) and simmer on low heat for 10 minutes.

2. Add the artichokes and continue to simmer for 5 minutes. The artichokes should be completely submerged: if they are floating above the surface, put a small plate or saucer on top of them to keep them under the surface.

3. Lift the artichokes from the cooking liquid with a slotted spoon and let them drain upside down on several layers of paper towels. When they are completely cool place them in one or more glass jars (choose jars with good lids) and add the parsley and marjoram. Pour in enough olive oil to cover the artichokes completely. Cover the jars and let the artichokes marinate at least 24 hours and up to 1 week in the refrigerator before serving them.

||||||||||||||||

RECIPE NOTES

To serve these artichokes as part of an antipasti, lift the artichokes from the marinade, letting most of the oil drain away. Set them out in dishes with the rest of the antipasti offerings. These artichokes are also great in salads or as a topping for bruschetta.

OLIVE OIL

IN GREEK MYTHOLOGY, Athena gave this luscious drupe to mankind as a gift—and, in gratitude, citizens of Attica were said to have named the city of Athens after her.

Because olive trees are native to the Mediterranean, the vast majority of unique preparations for olives are Mediterranean in nature. Essentially, olives break down into two types: green olives, which are picked while they are young for a denser, aggressive flavor, and black olives, which are picked when they are more mature. Olives also must be cured before being eaten, and can be dry cured, oil cured, salt cured, brined, water cured, or treated with lye before brining, like *Lugano* olives, a salt-cured variety. Some olives are cured and packed with herbs, such as the *Toscanelle* olive. Italians also make *Cerignola* olives, which are a sweet olive in both green and black renditions.

Olive oil can be fruity, nutty, sweet, zesty, peppery, rich, intense and assertive; mild, mellow, light or heavy, subtle and delicate; opaque or clear, deep olive green, pale green, gold-green, golden, or pale yellow. Like wine, no two olive oils are exactly alike.

Frantoio olives grown Tuscany and central regions of Italy are relatively big and when ripe they are a reddish-purple. Oil extracted from this olive is of high quality with a fruity and aromatic flavor. *Moraiolo* olives, grown in Tuscany and Umbria, are small and round and black when ripe. This olive produces a very good quality, fruity olive oil, with a green color. *Carolea* olives from Calabria, in the south of Italy, produce a medium-body fruity, golden oil.

The finest oil has the lowest free acidity. Virgin olive oil that has a free acidity of not more than 1% and has a noticeable fruitiness is classified as "extra virgin olive oil."

The most widely marketed grade of olive oil is simply labeled "olive oil." This oil is a blend of refined olive oil and virgin olive oil. The amount of virgin olive oil in a blended oil varies, depending on the flavor desired by the producer.

Choosing Olive Oil

The extra virgin olive oils of small producers vary in taste from year to year, much like wines do. You can conduct an olive oil tasting the same way you would a "blind" wine tasting. Record your impressions as you taste your way through three of four oils.

Before you taste each olive oil, look at the color of the liquid. Next, smell each oil, noting any aroma—the smell of olives—and bouquet— the "nose" of the oil. Professional olive oil tasters often rub a small amount of olive oil on their wrists to get a full sense of the oil's bouquet. Taste the oil using either a non-reactive spoon or a piece of bread. Finally, and perhaps most importantly, ask yourself: Do I like this oil?

Melanzane in Agrodolce (Caponata)

Sweet and Sour Eggplant Antipasto

YOU CAN FIND many variations of this recipe popular throughout southern Italy. It is frequently served on toasted bread, with grilled fish dishes, or to top fresh ricotta. In Puglia, this dish is served with panelle, a chickpea-flour-based "polenta" that can be fried or cooked in a pan like pancakes. I like it served with Farinata Ligure, a chickpea flatbread (see page 65).

SERVES 6

5 cups large-dice Italian eggplant, seeded before dicing

1 cup mild olive oil

2 cups small-dice red onion

1 cup celery, peeled and sliced

1½ tsp salt-cured capers, rinsed, and roughly chopped

2 tsp chopped black olives, pitted, roughly chopped

2 tsp tomato paste

1 tsp sugar, or to taste

3 tsp red wine vinegar, or to taste

1½ cups canned peeled tomatoes, lightly crushed

2 tsp chopped basil

Salt and freshly ground black pepper, as needed

1½ tsp pine nuts

1. To draw out the moisture from the eggplant, place it in a colander, salt well, and allow it to drain for at least 2 to 4 hours. Rinse the salt from the eggplant, and pat dry with paper toweling.

2. Heat ¾ cup of the oil in large skillet over medium-high heat, reserving the other ¼ cup for later use. When oil is hot, add the eggplant and cook until lightly browned on all sides. This is best done in batches so the eggplant takes on a good color; if you add too much to the pan at once, they won't brown. (Note: You may also fry them in a fryer; make sure to dust them with flour before deep-frying and work in small batches.) Transfer them to a pan lined with paper towels to blot briefly before you put them in a mixing bowl.

3. Wipe out the pan used for the eggplant, add the remaining oil, and return it to medium heat. Add the onions and cook for 10 minutes until translucent. Add the celery and cook for 2 to 3 minutes. Be sure the celery stays crunchy. Stir in the capers and olives. Add this mixture to the eggplant and toss well to combine. Set aside.

4. Once again, wipe out the skillet and return it to medium-high heat. Add the tomato paste and cook, stirring frequently, for 2 to 3 minutes. Add the sugar and vinegar. Stir until the sugar is dissolved. Add the crushed tomatoes and simmer over low heat for 10 minutes.

5. Pour the eggplant mixture into the skillet, add the basil, and stir to combine well. Taste and season with salt and pepper. Top with the pine nuts. Serve warm, room temperature, or cold.

Cipolline Borretane

Baby Onions in Olive Oil and Balsamic Vinegar

CIPOLLINE ARE SMALL, button-shaped onions that are very popular in Italy. Small shallots may be used instead if you can't find cipolline in your market; you might have to cook them a little longer, depending on their size. Use an average-quality (but still *tradizionale*) balsamic vinegar in this dish and save your best-quality balsamic to enjoy in other dishes.

This traditional Italian pickle could be put up in large amounts—in glass jars with a hermetic seal for long-term storage, in a cool, dry pantry—but this recipe is for a smaller batch that will last for up to three weeks in your refrigerator.

SERVES 6, MAKES 2 PINTS

2 lb cipolline onions	1½ cups red wine vinegar	1 tsp black peppercorns
2 cups average-quality balsamic vinegar	1½ cups mild olive oil	2 bay leaves
	1 tbsp kosher salt	

1. To blanch the onions, bring a large pot of salted water to a rolling boil. Add the onions and boil for 2 minutes. Immediately drain them and peel away the thin outer layers. Set them aside.

2. Combine the vinegars, oil, salt, peppercorns, and bay leaves with the onions in a large, stainless steel or enameled cast iron pan. Bring to a simmer over low heat and continue simmering for about 5 minutes, or until the onions are just tender; you don't want them to be overcooked. Use a slotted spoon to lift the onions from the cooking liquid and transfer them to clean glass jars. Fill the jars all the way with the hot cooking liquid until the onions are completely covered.

3. Add the lids to the jars and screw them in place. Set the jars upside down on a tray or the counter. As the onions cool, a slight vacuum will develop that helps preserve them. You may even hear a pop as the lids form a tight seal. Once cool, turn the jars right side up and store in the refrigerator. Let them "pickle" for at least 2 days before serving them. Use within 2 to 3 weeks.

BALSAMICO TRADIZIONALE

Make sure you use the real thing whenever a recipe specifies *balsamico tradizionale*. By law there are no imitations allowed when the word *tradizionale* appears on the label. And there really is no comparison between true balsamic vinegar and commercially sold imitations. Expect to pay about $20 to $35 per ounce if it is true balsamic vinegar. Good balsamic vinegar is made from wine must. Commercial varieties are often made from a red wine vinegar that has been mixed with caramel to give it more flavor and body. Read the ingredients on the back of the label and look for a trustworthy source.

PARMIGIANO OR GRANA CHEESE

There are several important Italian grating cheeses; the most familiar is what you may think of simply as "Parmesan." Parmigiano-Reggiano, Pecorino Romano, Grana Padano, and Pecorino Toscano are all different styles of aged grating cheeses. The quality of the cheese you buy matters a great deal. To be sure you are getting a quality product, look for the DOP on the packaging or ask the shopkeeper. DOP means that the product has been produced in accordance with specific standards and was made in a particular region of the country. These cheeses do not all taste the same, however, so try a few varieties to see which ones work best for you in a given dish. Sometimes, you need a really salty, sharp Pecorino, but other times you might prefer something a little more mild and nutty tasting.

Pera Dorata con Parmigiano e Balsamico

Caramelized Pear with Parmigiano-Reggiano Wedges and Balsamic Vinegar

I LIKE THE flavor and texture of perfectly ripe Anjou pears, but you can use any variety that is in season and that you enjoy. Choose the best quality Parmigiano or grana (Grana Padano, Emmental, or Gruyère) cheese and balsamico for this dish.

SERVES 6

3 Anjou pears, or your favorite variety	*¼ cup sugar, or as needed, depending on the pears*	*6 small wedges Parmigiano-Reggiano or Grana Padano*
¼ cup butter or mild olive oil		*6 tsp best-quality balsamic vinegar*

1. Peel, core, and cut the pears into 12 wedges. Melt the butter in a large sauté pan over medium-high heat. Add the sugar and pear wedges (make sure they are not overlapping or too crowded in the pan) and cook until the pear wedges are lightly browned, 3 to 4 minutes. Turn and brown the second side, another 2 or 3 minutes. Remove the wedges to a pan lined with paper towels to blot briefly.

2. Serve the pear wedges on individual plates or on a platter with the cheese wedges on the side. Just before serving, pour a teaspoon of the balsamic vinegar over each serving of pears. (Note: If your pear is perfectly ripe, you may serve them without cooking them first.)

ITALIAN CHEESES

THERE IS AN ASTONISHING ARRAY of flavorful and distinctive cheeses to be found in Italian gastronomy. Wines, sausages, dried foods, and cheeses are all the fruits of preservation practices known to ancient humankind, then refined, recorded, and evolved over time. We know that cheeses were enjoyed by the ancient Sumerians, whose writings about many aspects of daily life are believed to date from 3000 B.C.E. Early records of cheese have been found on earthenware vessels from Egyptian tombs dating as far back as 2300 B.C.E. The Bible includes numerous references to cheese, beginning with Genesis. Later in the Bible, David is said to have carried ten cheeses to the troops just before slaying the giant Goliath.

The Romans were the first to mass-produce cheese to be carried on long journeys and used by their armies as a convenient form of concentrated nutrition. They carried their formulas into conquered lands as their empire expanded, marrying them with indigenous cheeses in Europe. During the period of European history known as the Dark Ages, the traditions of cheese making were preserved and refined by religious houses and monasteries, as were the traditions of wine and spirit making. Some of these religious orders are still creating handmade cheeses using the same original formulas and methods.

Until the early to mid-1800s, cheese production continued on an individual home or cottage level by families who were fortunate enough to own sheep, goats, and cows. As farms grew in size and were able to supply communities with agricultural products, so the cheese business grew as well, although the cheese-making process continued to be both painstaking and time-consuming.

Cheese Making

The techniques used today to produce cheese have changed little since the times of the Romans and the medieval monasteries, but scientific

discoveries have led to better control of the natural processes involved in cheese making: acidification and coagulation of the milk, salting, cutting and draining the curds, shaping the cheese, and finally, ripening.

INGREDIENTS

Considering how few ingredients are needed to make cheese, there is an astonishing variety in the types of cheeses that can be produced. Hundreds of distinct cheeses can be made by introducing only slight modifications: Choosing sheep's milk instead of cow's, using a different starter culture, draining the cheese a little more or less, cutting the curds very fine or leaving them whole or in slabs, rubbing the cheese with salt at a different point in the process, even the choice of shaping it into a disk, a wheel, or a round, all will result in different cheeses, each with a unique texture, flavor, and aroma.

The type of milk the cheese maker chooses is critical to the development of the cheese. Not only are there different milks (cow, sheep, goat, yak, llama, buffalo, mare, and others), there are also various ways to collect, combine, and treat milk. One of Italy's most famous cheeses, Parmigiano-Reggiano, for instance, is traditionally made by combining the richer milk collected in the evening with the leaner milk of the next day's first milking.

SHAPING

There are a number of methods for draining and shaping cheeses, each specified both by tradition and by the role that those methods play in producing the desired flavor and texture in the finished cheese. After the curds are drained of the freed whey, some are placed in cheesecloth bags, baskets, or molds, and set on racks or hung and allowed to drain and dry for the prescribed time. For fresh and soft cheeses, draining and shaping is accomplished simultaneously.

RIPENING

The last stage of cheese making is ripening, also known as aging or curing. This is where the "magic" of flavor development takes place. The ripening process may take anywhere from 30 days to several years, depending upon the cheese being made. During that time, the cheese undergoes changes that will affect its flavor, body, texture, and occasionally its color. What began as rubbery fresh cheese curd is transformed into smooth and mellow ripened cheese.

Cheeses were originally aged in caves, where conditions were perfect for the magic of ripening to take place. Today, most cheeses are aged in temperature- and humidity-controlled environments that simulate caves.

Cheeses may be ripened in leaves, ashes, wax rinds, or no rind at all. Some are rubbed or washed, and some are simply left to cure naturally. In some cases, holes are made in the cheeses to allow gases produced by bacteria to escape; in others, the gases are confined to form a variety of holes ranging in size from tiny to the size of a quarter, as in Swiss cheese. Special additional bacteria cultures or molds are introduced in many cheeses by injecting, spraying, or washing them. Once these steps are done, the rest of the work is left to nature.

Cheese Classifications

For the sake of discussion, this section presents several broad groups of cheese that have been loosely categorized according to texture.

SOFT FRESH CHEESES

Soft fresh cheeses are those cheeses that are unripened and generally have a fresh, clean, creamy flavor. These cheeses are typically the most perishable and are sometimes held in brines.

Ricotta cheese, made from recooking whey, actually began in Italy as a by-product of the cheese-making industry. (The name literally means "recook.") When whey is heated, the proteins fuse together and create a new curd that, when drained, becomes a snowy white ricotta high in moisture and naturally low in fat. It is commonly used in Italian cooking as a filling for pastas or as a base for cheesecakes. Today, some ricottas are made with added part-skim or whole milk for a richer flavor.

Mascarpone is a fresh cheese made by curdling heavy cream with citric acid. The process releases excess moisture and yields a rich creamy cheese that is mildly acidic and adapts to both sweet and savory preparations. One of the most famous uses of mascarpone is in the dessert tiramisu, in which the rich cheese is layered with sponge cake or ladyfingers that have been dipped

in espresso and Marsala wine. Savory mascarpone dishes such as dips and spreads may also include herbs and spices.

SEMI-SOFT CHEESES

Semi-soft cheeses include a wide variety ranging from mild and buttery to very pungent and aromatic. They are allowed to ripen in several ways.

RIND-RIPENED CHEESES

Wash-rind cheeses are periodically washed with brine, beer, cider, wine, brandy, or oils during the ripening period. This remoistening encourages bacterial growth, sometimes know as a "smear," which allows the cheese to be ripened from the outside in. Popular examples of this type of cheese include Muenster, Tellagio, and Fontina.

Dry-rind cheeses are those that are allowed to form a natural rind during ripening. Bel Paese ("beautiful country") has become quite popular since it was first made in 1929. Its soft texture and very mild flavor have contributed to its popularity. Caciocavallo is a bottle- or pear-shaped cheese with a strong aroma but a mild taste. Asiago is one of the best known Italian waxed-rind cheeses.

BLUE-VEINED CHEESES

Blue or blue-veined cheeses are thought to have been among some of the first cheeses produced. Although there is no specific research to prove the theory, it is believed that the mold was first introduced to cheese from moldy bread that had come in contact with the cheese.

In the modern production of blue cheeses, needles are used to form holes that allow gases to escape and oxygen to enter to support mold growth within the cheese. The cheese is then salted or brined and allowed to ripen in caves or under "cavelike conditions."

Gorgonzola is the most widely known Italian blue cheese. Unlike it's French counterpart, Roquefort, made from sheep's milk, Gorgonzola is made from cow's milk, and the mold used to inject the cheese comes from a completely different strain. Gorgonzola is made with evening milk and the following day's morning milk. There are two varieties available: "sweet," which is aged three months, and "naturale," which is aged further and has a fuller, more robust flavor.

PASTA FILATA CHEESES

Pasta filata literally means "spun curds" or "spun paste." During manufacture, the curds are dipped into hot water and then stretched or spun until the proper consistency and texture is achieved. They are then kneaded and molded into the desired shapes.

Pasta filata cheeses are a group of cheeses that are related by the process used in their manufacture, rather than by their textures. In fact, the textures of pasta filata cheeses run the gamut from soft to hard, depending upon how they are aged, if at all.

The most common cheese of this category is mozzarella. Today there are two types of mozzarella available: the traditional fresh style, which is available in a variety of shapes and sizes, and the newer American invention of low-moisture mozzarella, which has a longer shelf life than the fresh style. Both whole milk and part-skim varieties are available.

Provolone is another popular pasta filata cheese that is similarly handled but is made with a different culture. Once the curd is stretched and kneaded, it is rubbed with brine and tied into shape. It is then hung and left to dry in sizes ranging from 250 grams to 200 pounds. Provolone is often smoked and/or aged for additional character and firmer texture.

VERY HARD CHEESES

In Italy, these cheeses are known as the *granas*, or grainy cheeses, because of their granular texture. The most popular of these cheeses are Parmesan and Romano, which are now produced in the United States and South America, but are different from their predecessors. Very hard cheeses are most often grated or shaved, but they are also traditionally eaten in chunks broken off with a special knife.

True Parmigiano-Reggiano is often referred to as the king of cheeses. It is believed that the formula for this cheese has not changed in more than 700 years, and its origins date back even further. This legendary cheese is made slowly and carefully following strict guidelines that require it to be aged a minimum of 14 months, although most are aged for 24 months. Stravecchio, or extra aged, is ripened for as much as three years.

The flavor of Parmigiano-Reggiano is complex and unique. Steven Jenkins, author of *The Cheese Primer*, describes it as "spicy like cinnamon or nutmeg; salty like liquor accompanying an oyster; sweet like ginger cookies; and nutty like black walnuts—all at the same time."

Romano cheeses—named for the city of Rome—come in several different varieties. Pecorino Romano, made with sheep's milk, is probably the best known. Caprino Romano is a very sharp goat's milk version, and Vacchino Romano is a mild version made from cow's milk.

Mozzarella Fior di Latte con Pesche e Prosciutto

Soft Fresh Mozzarella with Grilled Peach and Prosciutto

ARRANGE THE SLICED mozzarella on individual plates or on a large platter before you grill the peaches, because you want to serve the dish while the peaches are still hot.

SERVES 6

1 lb fresh mozzarella in water (this is a must!)

4 white peaches (or a good locally grown variety, preferably organic), firm and ripe

4 tsp extra-virgin olive oil

12 slices imported prosciutto (or sub-stitute coppa or culatello, found in specialty Italian markets)

4 basil leaves, thinly sliced

12 baby arugula leaves, washed and spun dry, for garnish

Juice of ½ lemon, or to taste

Salt and freshly ground black pepper, as needed

1. Slice the mozzarella so that you have about 2 slices per person, and arrange the slices on a large platter or 6 plates.

2. Preheat a grill to medium-high or heat a dry cast iron skillet over medium-high heat. Cut the peaches in quarters, removing the pit. Toss the quartered peaches with a few drops of the olive oil and place them on the grill or in the pan until they are very hot and a light brown on both sides, about 3 minutes total. Transfer the peaches to the platter or plates.

3. Drape the prosciutto on top of the peaches. Sprinkle some basil on top of the mozzarella.

Toss the arugula with a little lemon juice, a tea-spoon of the olive oil, salt, and pepper. Scatter the arugula on the platter or plates and drizzle the remaining olive oil on top of the mozzarella. Serve at once.

IIIIIIIIIIIIIIII
RECIPE NOTES

When peaches aren't in season, there are several good substitutes: melons, persimmon or pears. One more suggestion, which is really out of the ordinary, is a ripe mango. It may not be so Italian, but mango pairs nicely with the saltiness of the prosciutto and the delicacy of the mozzarella.

ABOUT MOZZARELLA

Mozzarella is crucial in our recipes. Mozzarella "fior di latte" is a mozzarella made of cow's milk. The original moz-zarella, made in the south of Italy, is made from buffalo milk, and should be eaten before it is more than one day old, if you are a purist. The secret to any dish that calls for mozzarella is to have a good source. Choose the best you can find, don't even try to use one that is dry and hard. Make sure it is soft to the touch and moist, preferably one that you can buy at a specialty store that gets their mozzarella made fresh weekly—or even better, made daily.

FICHI CON MIELE PEPATO
AL DRAGONCELLO E CAPRINO SOFFICE

FIGS WITH GOAT CHEESE, PEPPERED-HONEY, AND TARRAGON

SERVE THESE SMALL bites as an accompaniment to a salad of arugula, radicchio, and endive, with a platter of grilled vegetables, or as a side dish with grilled lamb chops or duck. Just use your imagination! For the richest flavor, serve this dish at room temperature or slightly warmed. If you have prepared the figs in advance and stored them in the refrigerator, allow them to warm for 30 to 40 minutes before serving.

SERVES 6

¼ cup honey

1 tbsp chopped tarragon, leaves only

Freshly ground black pepper, as needed

12 fresh figs, green or black

½ cup fresh goat cheese

1. Mix the honey with the tarragon leaves and black pepper. Set aside.

2. Cut the figs in halves or quarters, depending on their size, and arrange them on a platter or individual plates. Spoon about 1 teaspoon of the soft goat cheese on top of each fig piece. Drizzle the pepper-tarragon-honey mixture over the goat cheese. Serve and enjoy!

ABOUT FIGS

Italians are passionate about their figs (*fica*, or *fichi* in the plural). In fact, there is a whole culture devoted to figs. Find the best quality fruits you get your hands on. There are different types of figs. My father used to pick the ones from the ground just after they had fallen, saying that "if they don't want to stay on the tree, it means they are ready to be eaten by us." He would even seek out the ones he noticed that the birds were picking on. I admit that I am not a big fan of eating a fig that has been previously pecked by a bird, but I guess in his day there weren't so many worries about avian flu!

Polpettine di Tonno

Tuna and Ricotta Patties

THIS IS A perfect appetizer for a summer meal. Serve the patties hot or at room temperature, with a little salad or some vegetables.

SERVES 6, MAKES 18 PATTIES

8 oz canned tuna in olive oil

8 oz fresh ricotta, well drained

1 egg, lightly beaten

1 tsp chopped parsley

3 tsp grated Parmigiano-Reggiano cheese

Salt and freshly ground black pepper, as needed

1 tsp thinly sliced chives or scallion

¾ cup finely ground bread crumbs, plus as needed for coating patties

Mild olive oil for frying, optional

1. Preheat the oven to 350°F.

2. Drain the tuna well and use a fork or your fingers to separate it into fine shreds. Add the ricotta and combine well with a fork. Add the egg, parsley, cheese, salt, pepper, and chives. Add the bread crumbs a little at a time until you get a mixture that can be pressed into a cake.

3. Form the mixture into 18 small patties and dredge them in breadcrumbs. Bake them on a parchment-lined or well greased baking sheet until the exterior is crisp and golden in color, about 20 minutes. Alternately, you may prefer to pan fry the polpettine in olive oil rather than bake them. To do that, heat about ¼ inch of a mild olive oil in a frying pan. Coat the polpettine very well with bread crumbs before you put them in the hot oil. Fry them until crispy on both sides, about 2 or 3 minutes on each side. Drain them on a rack or absorbent paper towel before serving.

4. Serve the polpettine hot, or let them cool to room temperature before serving.

||||||||||||||||||||||||||||||||||||||||||||||||

TINNED FISH: *TONNO* AND *SGOMBERO*

Look for good-quality, imported tinned fish that has been packed in olive oil, which you can find in specialty Italian food stores. *Tonno* is the Italian name for tuna. You might also try substituting canned mackerel, or *sgombero,* for this recipe.

FRESH RICOTTA

With more and more cooks demanding fresh, high-quality ingredients, it has become easier to find great fresh products including fresh cheeses like ricotta. Ricotta can be somewhat wet; drain it well for a couple of hours in a colander that you've lined with a coffee filter or even a clean dish towel. Set the colander in a large bowl to catch the liquid as it drains away.

Rissole

Stuffed Crispy "Ravioli" Snacks

ITALIANS ARE FRUGAL by nature and necessity. But who could complain when little scraps of this and that end up making such a delicious snack? Serve rissole on their own as a snack or as an appetizer accompanied with a salad.

SERVES 4

FOR THE DOUGH:

2¼ cups all-purpose flour

7 tbsp butter, room temperature

Pinch of salt

½ cup water, or as needed

FOR THE STUFFING

8 oz cooked meat (any type)

2 egg yolks

Fresh chopped herbs (oregano, thyme, marjoram, or other), as needed

¼ cup grated Parmigiano-Reggiano cheese

Salt and freshly ground black pepper, as needed

4 cups mild-flavored oil, or as needed for frying

1. Combine the flour, butter, and salt in a bowl. Add enough of the cold water to blend the mixture into a smooth dough. Mix the dough quickly to avoid overworking it. Gather the dough into a ball, cover, and let rest in the refrigerator at least 20 minutes before rolling it out. (This dough can be made ahead and stored, tightly wrapped, in the refrigerator for up to 2 days.)

2. Cut the meat into strips or dice, removing any fat or gristle. Use a meat grinder or a food processor to grind the meat. (If you are using a food processor, use the pulse button to run the machine in short bursts. The meat should look finely ground, but not pasty.) Transfer the meat to a bowl and use a wooden spoon to mix in the egg yolks, the herbs, and the cheese. Season to taste with salt and pepper; set aside.

3. Roll out the dough on a lightly floured surface to the same thickness as a silver dollar and cut it into 16 circles, about 3 inches in diameter. Place 1 tablespoon of the filling in the center of each circle of dough. Lightly brush the edges of the dough with a little water, fold the dough in half over the filling, and press the edges together to seal.

4. Add enough oil to a heavy saucepan to fill it to a depth of about 2 inches. Heat the oil over medium heat until it reaches 350°F. Add about 5 or 6 rissole to the hot oil and fry them until they are evenly browned, turning them to get an even color. Lift the rissole from the oil with a slotted spoon and let them drain on paper toweling. Continue frying the risssole in batches until they are all fried. Serve hot.

Branzino Tiepido in Insalata con Fagioli e Pesto

Striped Bass Salad with White Beans and Pesto

ANY FISH WITH firm meat will work for this recipe, even tuna steaks. If you do decide to use tuna, be careful not to overcook it.

SERVES 6

1½ lbs striped bass or snapper fillets, skin removed	1 cup dry white wine	Salt and freshly ground black pepper, as needed
6 tsp olive oil	2 tsp chopped parsley	½ cup Pesto (page 28)
1 tsp chopped garlic	20 oz cooked or canned white beans (cannellini, navy, etc.)	

1. Cut the fish into small cubes, about ¾ inch, and set aside.

2. Heat the olive oil in a sauté pan over medium-high heat. When the oil is shimmering and quite hot, add the fish and lightly sauté it for 2 or 3 minutes. Gently loosen the fish from the pan as it cooks to make sure it doesn't stick to the pan.

3. Add the garlic, wine, and parsley to the pan. Let the mixture cook for 1 minute, just until the fish is cooked through but still moist. Remove the pan from the heat and let the fish cool slightly.

4. Drain the beans (rinse well if using canned beans). Place them in a bowl and season with salt and pepper to taste. Add the pesto and toss the beans until they are coated.

5. Make a bed of the beans on a platter or individual plates, top with the warm fish, and serve at once.

||||||||||||||||||
RECIPE NOTES

If you are cooking the beans for this, start with 10 oz dry beans (about 2 cups). Make sure you soak the beans overnight. When you are ready to begin cooking, drain the beans and put them in a pot. Add enough water to come 2 to 3 inches above the beans.

Make a sachet by wrapping 2 springs of rosemary, 1 sprig of sage, and 3 cloves of garlic sliced in half in a small piece of cheesecloth. Tie or knot the sachet and add it to the beans. Bring the water to a simmer and cook the beans over low heat for about 45 minutes or until tender.

PESTO

WHEN MAKING PESTO, the best choice is the Genovese basil, with its small and tender leaves. You may use regular basil if that's what your market carries, just make sure it's very fresh. To check the freshness, rub a leaf between your fingers and sniff. You should experience a strong rush of scent. You can add a few raw spinach leaves in with the basil to brighten up the pesto's green color.

MAKES ½ CUP

1 cup packed basil leaves

3 tbsp pine nuts

1 garlic clove, peeled

6 tbsp extra-virgin olive oil

Pinch of coarse sea salt

¼ cup grated Parmigiano-Reggiano cheese

1. Clean the basil gently with a damp cloth to avoid bruising it.

2. Heat a small skillet over medium heat. Add the pine nuts and toast them for 2 to 3 minutes. As soon as they are a golden brown, pour them out of the pan onto a cool plate and let them cool. (Make sure the pine nuts don't become too dark, because this will make the pesto bitter.)

3. Add the basil, garlic, oil, and a pinch of coarse salt to a food processor or blender. Puree until a relatively even, but still coarse, paste develops. Add the pine nuts and continue to process until everything is well combined, dense, and creamy. If the pesto is too dry, add a tiny bit of water.

4. Transfer the mixture to a bowl, add the Parmigiano-Reggiano and stir in until combined.

Insalata Tiepida di Gamberoni e Finocchi

Warm Large Shrimp with Fennel and Arugula Dressing

BEANS ARE ALSO a good combination with shrimp if the fennel doesn't look the best when you are in the market. Make the recipe in same way, substituting the beans for the fennel in step 2. The method for preparing dry beans can be found on page 27. If you are using canned beans, buy a good quality bean, ideally organic and unsalted.

SERVES 6

4 large fennel bulbs

1 cup dry white wine

Juice of 1 lemon

3 sprigs parsley

8 whole black peppercorns

2½ lb large shrimp

2 garlic cloves, thinly sliced

¼ cup extra-virgin olive oil

ARUGULA DRESSING

1 bunch arugula (about 6 oz),
    cleaned and dried

½ cup roughly chopped parsley

8 large basil leaves

Juice of 1 lemon

¼ cup extra-virgin olive oil

Salt as needed

8 whole pink peppercorns, crushed,
    for garnish

1. To prepare the fennel, trim the stems at the top of the bulb and cut away a little of the root. Remove the outer leaves if they are bruised. Rinse the fennel in cool water and let them drain. Slice them lengthwise into thin slices, no more than ¼ inch thick.

2. Place the fennel slices in a large sauté pan with the wine, lemon juice, parsley sprigs, and peppercorns. Add enough warm water to barely cover the fennel. Bring this to a gentle simmer over low heat. Maintain the simmer until the fennel is slightly softened, about 10 minutes. Keep the fennel warm while you prepare the shrimp.

3. If the shrimp are not peeled and deveined, prepare them while the fennel cooks: Using a small knife, make a cut along the back of the each shrimp and remove the black part of it. Wash them in cold water.

4. Heat the garlic with the olive oil in a skillet over low heat for 2 or 3 minutes (the garlic should have an intense smell, but should not become too dark), add the shrimp and gently cook them until they are just done through and not overcooked, 3 or 4 minutes, depending upon the size. (Do this in batches if your pan cannot hold all of the shrimp at once.)

5. Place all the ingredients for the dressing in a blender, and let the machine run for few seconds until they come together and are well combined.

6. Remove the fennel from its cooking liquid (it should still be warm) and place on the plate; top with the warm shrimp, and drizzle with the arugula dressing. Just before serving sprinkle the dish with the crushed pink pepper.

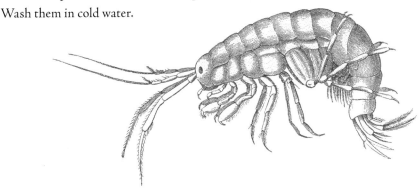

Calamari Fritti in Carpione

Lightly Pickled Fried Squid

IN THIS RECIPE, calamari are pickled after being fried. This dish is a great addition to an antipasti selection. Furthermore, if you have the opportunity to buy a significant quantity of fresh calamari, fry them all and enjoy some of them fresh and hot from the pan served with the classic accompaniments: a light plum tomato sauce, spicy if you like it that way, or a citrus-garlic-flavored mayonnaise (aïoli). Then, put the rest of the fried calamari into this pickle and store for a few days so they develop a great flavor. If fresh calamari isn't available, you can substitute sardines, bluefish, or whiting.

SERVES 6

2 lb squid, cleaned

½ cup extra-virgin olive oil

3 red onions, sliced about ⅛ inch thick

1 rosemary sprig

4 bay leaves (preferably fresh)

5 or 6 whole black peppercorns

2 cups red wine vinegar

3 qt oil peanut or canola oil, or as needed for frying

1 lb all-purpose flour, or as needed

Salt and pepper as needed

1. Wash the squid and cut the body into ½-inch-wide rings; leave the tentacles as they are.

2. Heat the olive oil in a large skillet over medium-high heat. Separate the onion slices into rings, add them to the olive oil, and cook for 2 to 3 minutes until they wilt. Add the rosemary, bay leaves, and whole peppercorns. Let the flavors develop together for 2 to 3 minutes, and then add the vinegar. Bring to a simmer, remove from the heat, and set aside.

3. Heat the peanut or canola oil in a deep pan to 375°F. (There should be about 2 inches of oil in the pan with at least 4 inches of space above the surface of the oil.) Dredge the squid in flour, shake off any excess, and immediately put the squid into the hot oil, making sure the pieces don't stick together.

4. When lightly crispy, about 4 to 5 minutes, remove the squid from the oil with a slotted spoon or spider and blot them briefly in a paper towel-lined pan. Season with salt while very hot.

5. Place a layer of the fried squid in a casserole or deep oval plate and pour some of the onion-vinegar marinade on top of the pieces. Continue making layers of squid and remaining marinade. Let the squid absorb the marinade for at least 1 hour before serving.

||||||||||||||||

RECIPE NOTE

If you use frozen squid, soak them in a little milk before dredging them in the flour.

Polipo a Fettine con Soncino e Finocchio

Thinly Sliced Octopus with Mâche and Fennel Salad

THIS IS ALSO called octopus carpaccio, for the way it is often presented. The trick for success with this dish is rolling the octopus up very tightly while it is still rather warm. If your octopus is very fresh, it might be naturally salted, so be sure you adjust the seasoning accordingly.

SERVES 6

3 lb octopus, fresh or frozen and
    defrosted

1 medium onion

1 medium carrot, peeled

1 celery stalk

2 garlic cloves, crushed

1 cup dry white wine

8 parsley stems

1 fennel bulb

¼ cup extra-virgin olive oil

Juice of 1 lemon

Salt and freshly ground black pep-
    per, as needed

2 cups packed mâche or baby arugula

1 dill sprig for garnish

1. Combine the octopus in a Dutch oven or flameproof casserole with the onion, carrot, celery, garlic, white wine, and parsley stems. Add enough cold water to cover the octopus by about 3 inches. Bring to a simmer over medium heat and cook for about 3 hours, or until the octopus is very tender. (Check for doneness by piercing the thickest part of the tentacles with a fork; the fork should slide in and out very easily.)

2. Once cooked, take the Dutch oven off the heat and let the octopus cool partially, but not fully. Pull off part of the red skin on the body of the octopus and clean the head. Lay a clean linen or cotton towel or large napkin on your work surface. Place the octopus on the cloth and wrap it so that it looks like a tube. Gather the cloth at each end of the tube and twist the cloth tightly (twist each end in opposite direc-

tions so you get a nice compact roll, similar to a salami). Cover well with plastic wrap and place the octopus in the refrigerator to cool completely, at least 4 hours or overnight.

3. When you are ready to serve the dish, clean the fennel, remove the hard core, and slice it very thin. In a salad bowl, toss the sliced fennel with 1 tablespoon of the olive oil, one tablespoon of the lemon juice, salt, and pepper, and set aside to marinate for about 20 minutes.

4. Toss the mâche or baby arugula with 2 tablespoons of the lemon juice, 2 tablespoons of olive oil, salt and pepper and place in the center of a platter or individual plates. Spoon some of the thinly sliced fennel on top of the mâche.

5. Remove octopus from the cloth and slice it very thin. Place the slices on top of the fennel, and top with the remaining olive oil and lemon juice, and garnish with a little piece of the dill.

CLEANING OCTOPUS

Octopus is typically sold already cleaned. However, you may need to occasionally remove the viscera, eyes, and beak (sometimes know as the eye). If the octopus you purchase has already been cleaned, simply cut the head away from the legs, and cut into the appropriate size. Baby octopus are typically cooked whole.

1. Use the tip of a filleting knife to cut around the eye and lift it from the octopus.
2. Peel the skin away from the body by pulling firmly.
3. Pull the suction cups away from the tentacles. The octopus is now ready to use.

CLEANING SQUID

When properly fabricated and cooked, squid is tender, sweet, and flavorful: The squid mantle can be cut into rings to sauté, pan fry, or deep-fry; or the squid may be left whole to grill or braise, with or without a stuffing. If desired, the ink sac can be saved and used to prepare various dishes, which will turn a dramatic black color.

1. Pull the mantle and the tentacles apart under running water. The eye, ink sac, and intestines will come away with the tentacles.
2. Pull away as much of the skin as possible from the mantle. Discard the skin.
3. Pull the transparent quill from the mantle and discard.
4. Cut the tentacles away from the head by making a cut just above the eye. If desired, the ink sac may be reserved. Discard the rest of the head.
5. Open the tentacles to expose the beak. Pull it away and discard. The tentacles may be left whole if they are small or cut into pieces if large.

Scarpetta ai Frutti di Mare con le Verdurine

Grilled Bruschetta with Warm Seafood Salad and Vegetables

TRANSLATED FROM ITALIAN, *scarpetta* means "little shoe." *Fettunta* is a variation of the typical bruschetta—they are both simply a grilled piece of bread topped with something. There is a saying that anytime you cook squid, you must cook it for either two minutes or twenty minutes. The two-minute squid will stay tender, but after the two minutes pass, it will toughen and you need to let it cook longer to become soft again, which usually takes twenty minutes, depending on the variety of the squid, its source, and its freshness.

SERVES 6

18 mussels

18 clams

½ cup extra-virgin olive oil

1 tbsp chopped garlic

1 cup dry white wine

1 lb squid

6 large sea scallops

1 tbsp minced shallot

1 celery stalk, white part only, cut into matchsticks

¼ cup chopped parsley

1 lb shrimp, 16-20 count, cleaned and deveined

1 cup halved grape tomatoes

2 tbsp torn basil leaves

Juice of 1 lemon

Salt and freshly ground black pepper, as needed

6 large slices bread, such as ciabatta or any good Italian bread

1 garlic clove, halved

½ cup thinly sliced radishes

1. Wash the mussels and clams thoroughly. Remove the beards from the mussels.

2. Heat half of the olive oil in a sauté pan over medium-high heat with half of the garlic. When the garlic is aromatic, about 2 minutes, add the clams and mussels along with half of the wine. Let simmer over low heat, covered, until the clams and mussels are opened, 8 to 10 minutes. Once opened, remove them from the pan, pull the meat from the shell, and reserve, discarding the shells along with any mussels or clams that do not open.

3. Clean and wash the squid. Cut the squid's body into small rings, and cut the tentacles in half lengthwise. Remove the muscle tabs from the scallops.

4. Heat the remaining oil over medium heat with the shallot and the remaining the garlic. Once the shallot and garlic develop some of their flavor and are fragrant, about 2 minutes, add the celery and half of the parsley (make sure it is very fresh, and preferably still wet after you wash and chop it).

5. Add the seafood in this order: calamari

first, then the shrimp, and finally the scallops, letting each type of seafood cook for a minute or two before adding the next. Add the remaining wine and the tomatoes and let cook for 3 or 4 minutes until the shrimp and scallops are cooked through. (Do not overcook the seafood, as it will toughen.)

6. Add the remaining parsley, the basil, lemon juice, salt, and pepper. Drizzle with some more extra-virgin olive oil and set aside.

7. Toast the bread on a grill or under a broiler or salamander until the outside is lightly colored, but the inside still quite soft. Rub each bread slice with a piece of halved garlic, place the seafood on the bread, and top with some radish slices.

|||||||||||||||||

RECIPE NOTES

You may try using different varieties of fish for this dish. Here we listed the most common ones: mussels, clams, shrimp, and scallops. You can also substitute lobster, baby octopus, oysters, and any firm white fish cut into small pieces.

Pane Cunziato (Bruschetta) ai Tre Sapori

Bruschetta with Three Different Toppings

THE BEST WAY to enjoy this piece of bread is as simple as this: choose an appropriate bread, grill it at just the moment you are ready to enjoy it, leave the inside soft and the outside not too hard. Good olive oil is a must; after that, it's whatever your heart tells you. Here are some ideas: chicken liver, grilled beef, cauliflower, broccoli, kale (I recommend Lacinato), roasted beets with goat cheese, chickpeas with olive paste, beans with grape tomato and a hint of truffle oil, meat of any kind (especially if it has been braised and then pulled, or grilled and thinly sliced), escarole, lentils, eggplant, peppers, zucchini, and any kind of seafood from grilled to braised.

I made this recipe easy to put together, without the hassle of cooking your own legumes or making your own olive purée. Organic canned chickpeas work great, just drain and rinse them. For the mushrooms, porcinis, chanterelles, or morels are my favored choices, but, of course, you can just see what the market has to offer for the money you have in your pocket.

SERVES 4 TO 6

BROCCOLI RABE TOPPING

1 lb broccoli rabe

¼ cup extra-virgin olive oil

3 garlic cloves, crushed

¼ tsp hot pepper flakes, as needed

Salt and freshly ground black pepper, as needed

¼ cup dry red wine

MUSHROOM-ASPARAGUS TOPPING

1 shallot, minced

2 tbsp extra-virgin olive oil

2 tsp chopped parsley

1½ cups sliced mushrooms

¼ cup white wine

1 lb white or green asparagus, peeled and blanched

2 hard boiled eggs, chopped

1 tsp chopped tarragon

1 tbsp lemon juice

CHICKPEA TOPPING

1½ cups chickpeas, cooked, unsalted, drained

1 tbsp prepared black olive purée (tapenade)

Salt and freshly ground black pepper, as needed

12 bread slices, preferably unsalted ciabatta

½ cup extra-virgin olive oil

1 garlic clove, halved

GARNISHES

Extra-virgin olive oil, as needed for topping bruschetta

¼ cup grated Parmigiano-Reggiano (for broccoli rabe topping)

3 oz fresh goat cheese, crumbled (for chickpea topping)

1. *For the broccoli rabe topping:* Rinse the broccoli rabe well, remove the hard stems, and cut into pieces small enough to fit on top of the bread slices. Heat the olive oil with the garlic and hot pepper flakes in a skillet over medium heat. Once the garlic starts getting a little bit of color, about 2 minutes, add the broccoli rabe, season with salt and pepper, and toss to coat evenly with the oil. Cook for 2 to 3 minutes, stirring frequently. Add the wine and finish cooking until soft, about 5 to 6 minutes more.

2. *For the chickpea topping:* Drain the chickpeas well and rinse in cool water if using canned beans. Toss them with the olive purée, salt, and pepper, and set aside. Garnish with goat cheese just before serving.

3. *For the mushroom-asparagus topping:* Preheat a grill to medium-high or the oven to 450°F. Heat the shallot with half of the oil in a sauté pan over high heat for 3 to 4 minutes. Add the parsley and mushrooms and cook for 1 minute. Add the wine and finish cooking the mushrooms until they are tender and flavorful, about 5 minutes. Place in a bowl and set aside.

4. Blanch the asparagus spears in a large pot of boiling salted water. Cut off the hard stems and then grill or roast them in the oven for 2 to 3 minutes until they are lightly browned. Slice them on a diagonal about ½ inch long and toss them with the mushrooms. Mix in half of the hard boiled eggs, the tarragon, lemon juice, and the rest of the oil. (Reserve the rest of the eggs to top the bruschetta just before serving.)

5. *To complete the dish:* Once the three toppings are ready, begin to get the bread ready. Brush the slices lightly with olive oil. Grill or broil the slices until golden on both sides but still soft on the inside. While they are still very hot, rub the garlic clove on each slice and set on a plate. Top each slice with the fillings and then add a garnish: For the broccoli rabe, sprinkle some Parmigiano-Reggiano cheese on top before serving. For the chickpeas, crumble some of the goat cheese on top. For the mushroom-asparagus, top with the remaining chopped egg. Enjoy.

||||||||||||||||
RECIPE NOTE

Broccoli rabe has a great, bitter flavor, which I like but you may not. To reduce the bitterness of the broccoli rabe, you may wish to blanch it first in a large pot of boiling salted water. Blanch for about 2 minutes, then drain, rinse in cool water, and squeeze to get rid of the excess water.

VIN COTTO

Vin cotto (cooked wine), *mosto cotto* (cooked must), and *saba* are all sweet vinegars that are used as sweeteners and condiments. They are made by cooking down the grape must left over from making red wine (winemakers refer to this sediment as the "lees"). These vinegars are sweeter than balsamic vinegar, but are used in much the same way.

INSALATA DI CAPUCCIO, MELA VERDE, NOCI AL VIN COTTO E ACETO DI MIRTO

CABBAGE SALAD WITH GREEN APPLE, WALNUTS, VIN COTTO, AND MYRTLE VINEGAR

MIRTO, OR MYRTLE, is a plant typical in Sardinian cooking. The name comes from the Greek, and the plant was considered sacred to Venere, *la dea dell'amore* (the love goddess). Both the leaves and berry pods (*bacche*) are used to make various products, including perfumes, digestives, and vinegars, and it is popular as an aromatic for cooking meats and fish.

SERVES 4 TO 6

1 small fresh heading cabbage, green, red, or a mixture

Salt and freshly ground black pepper, as needed

3 tbsp extra-virgin olive oil

⅓ cup toasted walnut halves

¼ cup *vin cotto* (see note on page 38)

2 firm, tart apples, green, red, or a mixture

2 tbsp myrtle vinegar (*aceto di mirto*)

1. Cut the cabbage in half, remove the hard core, and, using a mandolin or a very sharp knife, slice the cabbage very, very thin. Place the cabbage in large bowl, season with salt and pepper and 2 tablespoons of the oil. Set aside to rest for about 10 minutes; this will tenderize and flavor the cabbage.

2. Toast the walnuts while the cabbage rests, if you haven't already, and toss them together with the *vin cotto* in a small bowl. Set them aside.

3. Just before you are ready to serve the salad, core the apples and slice lengthwise into thin slices, no more than ¼ inch thick. Add the apples to the cabbage and toss them together. Add the remaining oil and the mirto vinegar and toss well. You could serve the salad directly in the bowl or make individual plates. Sprinkle some walnuts on top of the salad and enjoy!

RECIPE NOTES

Use a mixture of green and red cabbages and apples if you like more color contrast. Choose the freshest, most tender cabbage you can find—small and without too much core. A cabbage with too much core will feel heavy when you cradle it in your hands. To make sure a head of cabbage is fresh before you buy it, remove one of the outer leaves and try to break it. It should sound very crunchy. If you take a bite, it should be tender to the bite and more sweet than peppery.

Cavoletti alla Crudaiola con Mandarino, Melograno e Pignoli

Shaved Brussels Sprouts Salad with Clementines, Pomegranate, Pine Nuts, and Cheese

Salads like this, mixing fruit with vegetables, have become quite popular in Italy, including some made with vegetables that we wouldn't normally think of eating raw. Give it a try, you won't be disappointed, the combination is great.

SERVES 4

1 lb Brussels sprouts

1 medium carrot, very thinly shredded

½ cup pine nuts, toasted

Salt and freshly ground black pepper as needed

¾ cup Pecorino Romano or aged Asiago DOP, shaved

Juice of 1 lemon

¼ cup extra-virgin olive oil, mild

¾ cup clementine or orange segments

½ cup pomegranate seeds (about 1 fruit)

1. Choose very fresh Brussels sprouts. After partially removing the hard part at the bottom of the core, shave the Brussels sprouts very thinly with a mandolin, being careful not to break them up too much, and place into a bowl large enough to accommodate them. Shred the carrot into the bowl, then add the pine nuts, seasoning, half of the cheese, the lemon juice, and the olive oil and toss together.

2. Divide among 4 plates and garnish with the clementine or orange segments and the remaining cheese, and sprinkle the pomegranate seeds all over.

IIIIIIIIIIIIII
RECIPE NOTE

You may also add thinly shaved radishes or beets to this salad, but only add beets at the very end, to avoid them bleeding on the plate.

Insalata Pantesca

Pantesca Salad from the South

IF YOU HAVE extra guests coming over with little or no notice, mix in some greens just before you serve this, and, if you have some fresh mozzarella, add it as well. *Bocconcini* or *ciliegine* mozzarella are especially nice. If you are concerned about your guests biting down on the olive pits, you can pit the olives before you add them to the salad, but it isn't mandatory.

SERVES 6

2 lb Yukon gold potatoes, well scrubbed

Salt and freshly ground black pepper, as needed

2 pints grape or cherry tomatoes

18 Sicilian olives

1½ celery stalks, peeled and thinly sliced

1 medium red onion, sliced into thin rings

3 tbsp salted capers, rinsed

1 tbsp chopped parsley

1 tbsp chopped basil

2 tsp chopped oregano (fresh or dry)

12 oz canned mackerel or tuna, packed in oil

½ cup extra-virgin olive oil

Juice of 1 large lemon

1. Put the potatoes in a pan and add enough cold water to cover them completely. Put the pan on medium heat, add a pinch of salt, and bring the water up to a simmer. Cook the potatoes until they are tender, about 20 minutes depending upon the size of your potatoes; the tip of a paring knife will slide easily into the center of the potato when it is done. Don't overcook them, though, or they won't hold their shape in the salad. As soon as the potatoes are tender, drain them and let them cool. (Don't run cold water over them! Let them cool down on their own.)

2. As soon as the potatoes are cool enough to handle, slip off the skins (use a paring knife or a table knife if it doesn't come away easily). Cut the potatoes into pieces about the size of a medium olive and put them in a bowl.

3. Wash the tomatoes and cut them into easy-to-eat pieces. Add the tomatoes to the cooled potatoes along with the olives, celery, red onion, and capers. Mix in the herbs, taste the salad, and season with a little bit of salt and pepper to taste.

4. Flake the mackerel or tuna into pieces directly into the salad and dress the whole dish with the olive oil and lemon juice. Toss gently, trying not to break the fish apart too much. Serve this salad either at room temperature or lightly chilled.

||||||||||||||||||
RECIPE NOTE

Any heirloom or beefsteak tomatoes, firm and ripe, may be used, but be sure they are not overripe—they should have a good "bite," but not too soft. Replace the lemon with lime or vinegar for an even sharper taste.

Insalata di Riso

Rice Salad

THIS IS ONE of those recipes where you can improvise based on what you have in the refrigerator or dispensa (dry storage). You could replace the rice with a cooked pasta like orzo; substitute emmenthal or another cheese for the mozzarella; or add roasted or fried eggplant, beans, corn, pickled small onions, ham, shrimp or any other seafood, or whatever you'd like.

SERVES 6

1 cup superfine Arborio rice

Extra-virgin olive oil as needed

1 zucchini, diced small

½ cup fresh or frozen peas, blanched

2 roasted bell peppers, red and yellow

1 ball fresh mozzarella (about 3 oz), diced small

2 cups quartered cherry tomatoes

½ cup cold Tomato Sauce (page 102)

½ cup cured black olives, like Taggiasche, pitted and sliced

8 cornichons, diced very small

1 tbsp small capers, rinsed well

2 tbsp chopped parsley

2 tbsp chopped basil

Juice of 1 lemon

Salt and freshly ground black pepper, as needed

4 hard-cooked large eggs, quartered

1. Bring a large pot of salted water to a rolling boil over high heat. Add the rice, stir once or twice to separate the grains, and cook the rice until it is tender to the bite but not overcooked, 13 to 15 minutes. At once, drain the rice through a wire-mesh sieve and pour it onto a baking sheet. Drizzle a little olive oil on the rice and gently toss and fluff the rice to coat it with oil. Spread the rice in a thin layer, let it cool completely, and then transfer it to a bowl.

2. Bring a medium pot of salted water to a rolling boil over heat high. Add the diced zucchini and let it cook for about 30 seconds. Use a slotted spoon to lift the zucchini out of the water and into a colander. Rinse with cold water until it is no longer hot. Let the zucchini drain well in the colander or on a few layers of paper towels. Using the same boiling water, blanch the peas in the same manner. Cook fresh peas for about 1 minute; if your frozen peas aren't thawed, you may have to cook them a little longer.

3. You can use good-quality bottled roasted peppers or freshly roasted peppers. Fresh peppers can be roasted over a stovetop flame until blackened all over, then placed in a brown paper sack to steam for about 10 minutes. In both instances, remove the skin and any seeds that remain on the roasted peppers before using.

4. Dice the peppers and add them to the rice, along with the zucchini, peas, mozzarella,

cherry tomatoes, tomato sauce, black olives, cornichons, capers, parsley, and basil.

5. Dress the salad with a few generous pours of the olive oil, season with lemon juice, salt, and pepper. Toss the salad to combine it well. You can serve the salad right away or keep it in the refrigerator to serve several hours or up to two days later. I like to let it rest at room temperature for 30 minutes or so to take the chill off and open up the flavors.

6. Garnish with hard-cooked eggs immediately before serving.

ITALIAN RICE VARIETIES

All varieties of rice can be divided into short-, medium- and long-grain varieties. All Italian rice varieties are strains of a thick, short-grained rice called japonica (Oryza sativa japonica). They may not, to most palates, taste different, but they do behave differently when cooked. There are four grades of rice:

Comune or originario: The cheapest, most basic rice, typically short and round, used for soups and desserts, but never risotto.

Semifino: This grade, of medium length, maintains some firmness when cooked. Risotto can be made with a semifino grade, although semifino is better employed in soups.

Fino: The grains are relatively long and large and taper at the tips. Fino-grade rice remains firm when cooked. Several varieties are commonly graded fino, including Vialone Nano, Razza 77, San Andrea, and Baldo.

Superfino: This grade represents the fattest, largest grains. They take the longest to cook, and can absorb more liquid than any of the others while still remaining firm. Superfino rices include Arborio and Carnaroli.

PASSATELLI VERDI IN BRODO

PARMIGIANO-REGGIANO, SPINACH, AND LEMON DUMPLINGS IN BROTH

THIS DISH IS typical of Emilia-Romagna, and you will find different variations of this recipe throughout the region. Some omit the spinach or use different herbs rather than the ones I've given you here; one may have more Parmesan cheese and less bread crumbs, and so on.

SERVES 6

1 cup grated Parmigiano-Reggiano cheese

½ cup dry bread crumbs, homemade

½ cup spinach (or any greens), blanched and puréed

½ tsp finely grated lemon zest

¼ tsp freshly grated nutmeg

Salt and freshly ground black pepper, as needed

2 large eggs

2 large egg yolks

6 cups meat broth or chicken broth (page 49)

1. Combine the cheese, bread crumbs, spinach, lemon zest, nutmeg, salt, and pepper in a bowl.

2. In a separate bowl beat the eggs and egg yolks together. Add the eggs to the bread-parmesan mixture and combine until a good consistency is achieved. Place the mixture into a disposable pastry bag, filling it halfway, and set aside. You also may use a ricer, passing the mixture through the larger holes.

3. When ready to cook the dumplings, bring the broth to a simmer in a soup pot. Hold the pastry bag a few inches above the broth and squeeze or drop 2- to 3-inch-long dumplings directly into the broth. Simmer for about 1 minute over low heat. Serve very hot.

||||||||||||||||||
RECIPE NOTES

You need to get the feeling for the consistency of the mixture. If the dumplings fall apart in the broth, you might need to add more bread crumbs; if they are too dry, more eggs. There is a special tool sold just for making *passatelli,* but using a pastry bag is a very practical option. Another alternative is a food mill with large holes or a potato ricer.

Infarinata della Garfagnana

Tuscan Cornmeal Soup

GARFAGNANA IS HEARTY enough to be a full-course meal. If you have any left over (and you probably will), you may find that it tastes even better the next day. Should the soup get firm enough to slice, you can try something different: Slice it just as if it were polenta and fry or grill it to enjoy this soup all over again, but in a different form. Top with some soft cheese and serve with grilled meats.

SERVES 6

11 oz dry borlotti or cranberry beans	1½ lb Yukon gold potatoes	2 oz pancetta slices or thinly sliced salt pork
2 quarts water, or as needed	1 large red onion	Salt and freshly ground black pepper as needed
6 sage leaves	1 medium carrot	1 cup polenta, as needed
1 sprig rosemary	1 celery stalk	
4 garlic cloves, peeled	¼ cup extra-virgin olive oil	
1 lb Lacinato kale or savoy cabbage		

1. Sort, rinse, and soak the beans for at least 12 hours before starting the soup. Drain the beans and pour them into a soup pot. Add about 2 quarts of cold water, enough to cover the beans by 2 inches. Add the sage, rosemary, and 1 peeled clove of the garlic. Thinly slice the remaining peeled garlic and reserve for use in step 3. Put the pot over medium-low heat, cover it, and bring the beans to a gentle simmer. Let them cook until the beans are almost done, about 2 hours.

2. Meanwhile, wash the kale leaves thoroughly. Open each leaf and cut into 2-inch pieces. Trim and peel the potatoes, onion, carrot, and celery. Cut them into medium dice, roughly all the same size. Try to keep them separated, as you should add them to the soup pot in a specific order.

3. Heat the oil in a soup pot or casserole over medium heat. Add the onion to the olive oil and cook until it is limp and translucent, about 5 minutes. Add the celery, the carrot, the remaining garlic, and the pancetta. Once the vegetables start taking on a little color, about 6 minutes, add the kale and the potatoes.

4. Once the kale is wilted, add the beans and their cooking liquid. Add enough water to cover the vegetables, if needed. Season with salt and pepper and, as soon as the soup starts simmering slowly, add the polenta, a little at a time, while stirring constantly.

5. Let cook for about 30 to 40 minutes until soup is quite dense, but still soupy. Adjust the consistency with water, if necessary (this will depend on the quality and coarseness of the polenta). Just before serving, drizzle with some extra-virgin olive oil and a good amount of freshly ground black pepper, to taste.

Brodo di Carne

Meat Broth

WHEN I WAS very young, the kitchen where my family used to prepare the food for the customers was very close to the entrance to our bedrooms, as the trattoria and house were joined together in one building. I have very fond memories of smelling the day's broth, starting very early and continuing throughout the morning until at least noon, when it was time to serve the guests. The leftover meat was on our family table for a few days afterwards. Near the end, when all of us were tired of having reheated meat every day, my mom would take whatever was left, grind it up, add eggs and some Parmesan, and form little *polpettine* (patties), which she would pan fry. We used to love them as a snack or between two pieces of bread as a quick sandwich.

Make sure you keep the broth at a very gentle simmer. You may omit the beef if you'd prefer a chicken broth. In the same manner you could substitute duck for the chicken, being sure to completely remove all the skin and fat.

MAKES 4 QUARTS

3 lb chicken	2 carrots, medium dice	Cloves or peppercorns, optional, as needed
1 lb lean beef shank	2 stalks celery or celeriac, medium dice	1 tbsp salt, plus additional as needed
3 lb meat or chicken bones	½ cup chopped tomato, fresh or canned	6 parsley stems
6 qt cold water		2 thyme sprigs
2 onions, medium dice		

1. Place the chicken, beef, and bones in a large pot and add the water. Cover with a lid and bring to a gentle simmer. As soon as the broth reaches the simmer, remove the lid and begin skimming the surface periodically.

2. Add the remaining ingredients except for the herbs. Partially cover the pot and bring it back to a simmer over low heat. Let cook for about 2½ hours. Remove the lid completely and taste. If necessary, add a bit of salt and cook for an additional 5 to 10 minutes, until a very full flavor is achieved.

3. Remove the meat and set it aside for another use. Add the herbs to the broth and let them steep for 3 to 5 minutes, then strain.

Minestra Maritata

"Married" Soup from Campania

IN ITALIAN WHEN we want to say that two things go well together, we might say, *si sposono bene* (they're well married)—or if you come from the south, you'd say that they're *maritati*. This combination of greens and meat in a clear broth certainly does work well, definitely *maritata*.

SERVES 6

½ small head savoy cabbage or
   Lacinato kale (about 1 lb)

½ bunch broccoli rabe

½ head Bibb lettuce

¼ lb chicory

2 oz pancetta, cut into small pieces

2 oz prosciutto skin

2 garlic cloves, peeled

1 medium Spanish onion, peeled
   and left whole

¾ lb pork ribs

¼ bunch parsley

1 bay leaf

2 sprigs thyme

2½ qt water

5 oz fresh Italian sausage, cooked,
   casings removed, and sliced

1 oz caciocavallo, cut into small
   pieces

¼ tsp chopped fresh hot pepper, or
   to taste

12 slices of bread, toasted or grilled

¼ cup extra-virgin olive oil

1. Clean and wash the cabbage or kale, broccoli rabe, lettuce, and chicory. Cut the greens into big pieces and mix them together; set aside.

2. Place the pancetta, prosciutto skin, garlic, onion, pork ribs, and herbs into a stock pot, along with enough cold water to cover everything by an inch. Add a little salt, bring to a simmer over low heat, and cook 1½ to 2 hours, until the ribs are cooked through. Remove the ribs, pick off the meat, and cut into coarse pieces.

3. Strain the broth; add back the cooked meats along with the sausage, and bring the soup back to a simmer over low heat. Add the cut-up greens to the pan and cook for 8 to 10 minutes; thegreens should still be firm. Add the caciocavallo and the hot pepper. Simmer for another 10 minutes. Remove whatever is left of the prosciutto skin, and serve each bowl of soup with toasted or grilled bread topped with a drizzle of good Tuscan extra-virgin olive oil.

PROSCIUTTO

There are two types of prosciutto: cooked and raw. *Prosciutto crudo* (raw prosciutto) has been made in Italy since Roman times; the name means, "dried of liquid." *Prosciutto di Parma*, is a cooked variety many Americans are familiar with. Each region has specific standards which must be met in order to be designated a Protected Denomination of Origin, or DOP Prosciutto. Each regional consortium has its own specific brand or trademark that should be visible on the ham itself. You'll find that some types are sweeter, some saltier, some darker, and some more delicately flavored.

Pappa col Pomodoro Gamberi

Bread-Tomato Soup with Shrimp

THIS TRADITIONAL TUSCAN dish is thought to be a healthy dish. In the old days when intestinal infections were quite common especially among young children, garlic was the most widely prescribed *farmaco* (medicinal). To convince their children to have lots of garlic, Tuscan mothers used to tell their children that the *pappa col pomodoro* would make them pretty. You'll find plenty of variations of this soup, but the common theme for all of them is garlic, tomato, bread, and basil. I like to add some quickly sautéed shrimp or a few baked mussels or scallops.

SERVES 4

1 ½ lb tomatoes

3 tbsp extra-virgin olive oil, plus as needed for the shrimp and garnish

5 garlic cloves, smashed

½ cup torn basil leaves

½ lb ciabatta bread, thinly sliced

Salt and freshly ground black pepper, as needed

4 cups meat broth (page 49) or vegetable stock

16 shrimp, medium size, peeled and deveined

1. Blanch the tomatoes for 30 seconds in boiling water, then shock them in cold water, remove the skin, most of the seeds, and roughly chop them. Set aside.

2. In a casserole heat the oil with the garlic over medium heat until lightly golden, about 6 minutes. Add ¾ of the torn basil and the tomatoes. Bring it to a simmer, let cook for 3 to 4 minutes, and then add the bread slices. Mix well and season with salt and pepper.

3. Add the broth and let simmer for another 6 to 10 minutes. Remove the casserole from the heat and let it rest for about 15 minutes. Just before serving the *pappa*, whisk it with a whip so that you break up the bread.

4. While the soup is resting, sauté the shrimp in some good olive oil. If you prefer, the shrimp can be poached. Season to taste with salt and pepper and keep them warm to serve on top of the soup.

5. Ladle the soup into warmed bowls, top each with 4 shrimp per bowl, garnish with some fresh basil, and a few drops of good olive oil.

||||||||||||||||
RECIPE NOTES

This soup takes only about 20 minutes to prepare if all your ingredients are of good quality. The ciabatta should be unsalted, if possible, and a few days old so that it is quite dry.

If your tomatoes are not of the best quality and ripeness, you might want to add an onion to this recipe. If so, it should be chopped and cooked very slowly in olive oil.

Zuppa di Trippa

Tripe Soup

THIS SOUP IS a traditional recipe cooked throughout Italy, although each region (if not family) boasts a different style. I know what you're thinking as you read this recipe, and maybe you'll never make it. But since we're being very traditional in these pages, I have to say that tripe is an ingredient that is still cooked and appreciated by young and old alike.

Growing up in Napoli I was exposed to tripe a lot. Of course, when I was a little kid, I had no idea what it was. To me it just tasted good. I did learn what it was eventually, and I still loved it. There are fond memories I treasure to this day of grocery shopping with my mother, an event that took place practically every day. We would often stop at a place called "Fiorenzano," a shop that sold everything the pig had to offer—tongue, nose, head, feet, tail, even the ears and the snout. You name it, they had it. My favorite was their boiled tripe that had been diced and dressed with lemon and then served on square of waxed paper. It was delicious!

SERVES 4

3 tbsp extra-virgin olive oil

½ cup small-dice onion

20 oz tripe, cleaned, blanched, and cut into medium dice

1 fresh bay leaf

1 cup dry white wine

¾ cup crushed tomatoes or tomato sauce

1 garlic clove, chopped

½ tsp finely grated orange zest

2 tbsp chopped Italian parsley

2 tsp chopped rosemary leaves

Salt and freshly ground black pepper, as needed

Pinch of hot pepper flakes

2 qt meat broth (page 49)

½ cup grated Parmigiano-Reggiano cheese

1. Put the oil and onion in a soup pot and cook over low heat until the onion is soft, 2 to 3 minutes. Add the tripe and the bay leaf to the onion and cook for 3 to 5 minutes. Add the wine and continue to cook until it evaporates, about 10 minutes.

2. Add the tomato, garlic, orange zest, parsley, and rosemary. Season with salt, black pepper, and hot pepper flakes.

3. Pour in the broth and cook very slowly over low heat for 2 to 2½ hours, or until the tripe is very soft and the soup is quite dense. Serve the soup very hot with some parmesan cheese on top.

Zuppa di Cacio e Uova con Erbetta di Campo

Wild Greens Soup with Egg and Pecorino Romano

THIS SOUP IS a remake of the classic *stracciatella*, which is also quite popular all over the world. Spinach is very often used in the classic *stracciatella*. I like the idea of using different greens, bitter or not, such as collard greens, Swiss chard, kale, mustard greens or dandelion greens instead of only spinach. Parsley or any other fresh herb may be added as well.

SERVES 4

1 lb wild greens, mixed or not

2 onions, julienne

¼ cup extra-virgin olive oil

4 cups chicken, beef or vegetable broth

3 large eggs

¼ cup grated Pecorino Romano

Salt and freshly ground black pepper, as needed

1. Boil the greens in plenty of hot salty water until almost cooked, 6 to 8 minutes. Drain well, coarsely chop them, and squeeze out most of the water. In a soup pot, sweat the onions with the olive oil over medium-low heat. When tender, but not colored, after 4 to 5 minutes, add the chopped greens and mix well. Pour the broth into the onions and greens, and bring to a simmer. In a separate bowl, beat the eggs with the grated Pecorino, and add the egg-cheese mixture into the broth. Bring to a simmer again for 1 or 2 minutes. Season with salt and pepper, if necessary. Just before serving, use a whisk to "whip" the broth. Serve immediately.

IIIIIIIIIIIIIII
RECIPE NOTE

Any wild greens from the fields will work in this soup. Some of the greens can be very bitter. A good tip is to let them soak in cold water for 1 hour; they will lose some of their bitterness. Green chicory, for example, has a very bitter taste that not everybody likes.

Pecorino Romano DOP is just a little milder and less salty than the one sold commercially. If you are not sure about the quality of the Pecorino Romano, replace it with a good aged Pecorino Toscano. Make sure it is aged, otherwise it is a little difficult to grate.

ZUPPA DI GARRETTO DI MAIALE

PORK SHANK SOUP

BEEF SHANK OR chicken legs and thighs may be also used. You can also try this soup with veal, mutton, or lamb. If you can't find a shank, you may use any part of the pork leg.

SERVES 4

1 cup dry chickpeas

1 cup dry borlotti or cranberry beans

1 pork shank (about 2 ½ lbs)

1 onion, medium dice

2 celery stalks, peeled and diced

1 carrot, peeled and diced

1 garlic clove, chopped

3 tbsp extra-virgin olive oil

2 qt cold water

1 cup thinly sliced savoy cabbage

Salt and freshly ground black pepper, as needed

4 slices toasted or grilled bread as an accompaniment

1. Sort, rinse, and soak the beans (use a separate bowl to soak each type of bean) for at least 12 hours before starting the soup. Drain the beans and put them into separate pots. Add about 1 quart of cold water to each pot (the water should cover the beans by 2 inches). Bring the 2 legumes to a simmer over medium-low heat for 30 minutes. Drain the beans and set aside.

2. In a third pot, combine the pork shank with enough cold water to cover it, and bring to a simmer over medium-low heat for about 10 minutes (this is done just to get rid of some of the fat and impurities in the shank). Remove the meat and set aside; discard the water.

3. In a soup pot, sweat the vegetables with the oil over low heat until soft, about 8 minutes. Add the shank, legumes, and cold water, and slowly bring to a simmer over low heat. Let simmer until the meat is very tender, about 40 minutes. Remove the meat and set aside. Add the cabbage and keep on simmering for another 10 minutes.

4. Cut or shred the meat into small pieces, removing the bone. Return the meat to the pot and simmer for another 5 to 10 minutes. Season to taste with salt and pepper. Serve hot with toasted or grilled bread.

*"O mangiar questa minestra
o saltar questa finestra."*

Either eat this soup or jump out this window.
(Take it or leave it.)

— ITALIAN PROVERB

A TASTE OF HOME

THE DISTINCTIONS IN GASTRONOMY from one region to another reflect the climate and geography of that area. The local dialect spoken might be different, the scenery could change from a beautiful coastline with crystal blue water, to a series of fertile green hills or high mountain peaks covered with snow.

Foods, flavors, and cooking techniques can differ within a 20-kilometer range. What a great scenario for discovering tremendous variety of new additions to your culinary repertoire! You can quite literally see, touch, smell, and taste the vibrant diversity of Italian culinary arts as you travel the breadth of the country. If you look up Italy in a culinary dictionary, "redundant" is definitely not a word you will find in the definition.

One thing that keeps regional cuisines unique, apart from the obvious differences in climate and geography, is the fact that Italians tend to be conservative and even closed-minded when it comes to changes in their own traditions. We don't necessarily all enjoy the same things. Of course, we do know about the abundance of different dishes, cooking techniques, specialty foods, and wines that are found throughout Italy as a matter of national pride. Even though physical barriers like mountains or distance that once used to keep traditions from mingling are no longer significant factors, there still is a barrier that exists between the various regions, cities, and little villages of Italy.

When it comes to things of the table, we Italians are completely faithful to the culinary traditions of our family or village. We take great pride in our local food and wines. Everyone claims that their traditional recipes are more authentic, their produce more fresh and flavorful, their cheeses and cured meats superior to any other. We believe supporting our local growers and producers helps promote a vibrant local economy. Just as important to us, perhaps more so, is the conviction that when we buy local fruits and vegetables, drink the local vino sfuso (table wines), we keep our ancient local traditions strong and vital.

Italians are not afraid to express an opinion when it comes to food, and we can be loud about it. As crazy as it may seem to others, the passion we have for food often results in heated arguments—everyone wants to be right about his or her style.

Each Italian household and their extended families claim to have the best cooks and the best recipes. We are openly biased when it comes to our own recipes or style of preparing food. We are proud of our own personal techniques and recipes, and guard them so jealously that a lot of times we won't share our secrets. Recipes are passed from generation to generation through a closed network of grandmothers, cousins, aunts, and sisters. Dishes are often shared among neighbors, but secrets are never given away.

My family lived in the city of Napoli, and we used to have an apartment in a very modern building that stuck out among the older ones in our neighborhood. My mother was friends with Signora Anna, who lived across from our building. Signora Anna made a masterful tomato sauce, one of the best I've ever had to this

day. Since she knew that I loved it, she would often invite me over for lunch or give my mom a plate with pasta and some of her tomato sauce, though she never gave my mother her recipe.

I remember that my mom wasn't crazy about the idea that I liked Signora Anna's sauce better then hers. She would justify the difference, insisting that the sauce was made with canned tomatoes instead of fresh ingredients, but for me the real reason behind the difference remains a compelling mystery.

Often I call upon my mother (the best chef ever!) for some guidance with a recipe. One thing for sure about family recipes, however, is that even though these cooks may have incredible ability, passion, and creativity when it comes to the food they prepare, they may not be the best at writing everything down in a detailed manner, especially cooks of my mother's generation. They can create a masterpiece in the kitchen, but when it comes to telling you how to do what they do, their actions speak louder than words.

I always search for the exact measurement or cooking time or the precise consistency when she explains things to me. Her answers always go like this:

"Add a little of this or that…"
"When it tastes right…"
"When it feels right…"

And so on. Unfortunately, this rarely satisfies my curiosity about my mother's kitchen secrets, and usually sets the scene for a loud argument—a typical Italian exchange over food!

CHAPTER TWO

PIZZE E PANI

Pizzas and Breads

PIATTONA CON FICHI, CAPRINO, ARUGULA E OLIO TARTUFATO

FLAT BREAD WITH FIG PRESERVE, GOAT CHEESE, ARUGULA, AND TRUFFLE OIL

PIATTONA **MEANS VERY FLAT.** This is one of those doughs that is so quick and easy to make, and will come together under even the most adverse cooking conditions. I came up with the idea for this dish when I was working in a restaurant and needed to create a menu that was reasonable in price, and where children could find some familiar and comfortable foods on the menu that are fun to eat. The best thing about this dish is that it can easily become a whole meal.

SERVES 6

FOR THE PRESERVES

1 tbsp extra-virgin olive oil

1 tbsp chopped shallot

1 cup chopped dried figs

1 tbsp chopped fresh rosemary

½ cup Marsala wine

½ cup water, or as needed

FOR THE DOUGH

1½ cups all-purpose flour

1½ cups bread flour

1 cup water

1 tsp kosher salt or sea salt

2 tbsp extra-virgin olive oil, plus more for oiling the pan

FOR THE TOPPING

1 cup soft goat cheese

1 cup loosely packed baby arugula leaves

1 tbsp white truffle oil

1. To prepare the preserves: warm the olive oil in a saucepan. Add the shallot and cook it over low heat until it "sweats," about 2 minutes. Stir in the figs, rosemary, Marsala, and water. Simmer until the figs are very soft, about 20 minutes. (If there is too much water, continue to simmer until the right consistency is achieved. The preserve should be dense, but not too thick.) Allow the mixture to cool somewhat and transfer to a food processor. Process until it has the consistency of marmalade. (The preserves can be stored in the refrigerator if you make them ahead, but be sure to let them warm up to room temperature while preheating the oven.)

2. To make the dough: using an electric mixer or food processor, mix the two flours with the water, salt, and olive oil until a stiff dough forms, about 5 minutes on medium speed. The dough should be firm, smooth, and elastic. *(recipe continues on page 64)*

Divide the dough into six 4-ounce balls, set them on a lightly floured work surface about 2 inches apart, cover with a clean towel, and let rest for at least 30 minutes. Flour a work surface. Working with one ball of dough at a time, use the palm of your hand to flatten the dough. Use a rolling pin to roll it out as thin as possible (thinner than pizza), depending on how crunchy you like your piattona. Sprinkle the dough with flour and set it aside. Roll out the remaining balls of dough in the same way and set them aside as well.

3. Place a pizza stone in the cold oven (alternatively, oil a sheet pan and set it aside.) Preheat the oven to 450°F.

4. Place a piece of dough on the stone or baking sheet, and bake until the dough no longer sticks to the surface, about 2 minutes. (It is not fully baked at this point.) Remove and set aside. Repeat with the additional pieces of dough.

5. When you are ready to serve, spread some of the preserve on top of the partially cooked dough, and top with some of the goat cheese. Place in a 450°F oven and bake until the cheese starts melting and the bottom of the piattona is crispy, 1 to 2 minutes.

6. Transfer each piattona to a plate. Distribute some of the arugula leaves on top and drizzle with a few drops of the truffle oil. You can cut each piattona into wedges, or serve them as whole, individual "pies."

||||||||||||||||
RECIPE NOTES

You can partially cook the piattona as described in step 4 the day before you plan to serve them. Let the piattona cool and then wrap them well in plastic wrap and store in the refrigerator.

While I've given you some specific suggestions in this recipe, don't let that hold you back from trying your own combinations: pureed eggplant, beans or potatoes; a variety of different kinds of tomatoes, olives, capers, fresh or grilled greens such as radicchio, arugula, or endive; cooked shrimp or scallops, or smoked meats or fish like smoked salmon, all would be great.

Farinata Ligure

Chickpea Flatbread from Liguria

FARINATA IS A thin, crisp, pizza-like "bread" made from chickpea batter. This recipe makes three *farinate*, each large enough for two servings. The traditional pan used to make farinata is typically made of copper, but a well-seasoned, deep cast-iron skillet (sometimes known as a "chicken fryer") will work equally well.

SERVES 6

1¼ cups chickpea flour, sifted

1½ cups cold water

1½ tsp kosher salt

5 tbsp extra-virgin olive oil, plus
extra for oiling pan

¼ cup thinly sliced scallion, white
part only

¼ cup chopped fresh flat-leaf parsley

20 black olives, pitted

25 fresh sage leaves, coarsely
chopped

2 tbsp chopped fresh rosemary

1. Preheat an oven to 550°F.

2. Whisk the chickpea flour and water together until smooth. Add the salt and 3 tablespoons of the oil. Let rest for at least 45 minutes at room temperature (the batter can be made the night before). Remove any foam that forms on the top with a slotted spoon and discard.

3. Warm 2 teaspoons of the remaining olive oil in a sauté pan over low heat, and sauté the scallion until it is soft, about 3 minutes. Add half of the parsley and set aside.

4. To make the first farinata, put the cast iron skillet in the oven, and allow it to preheat. Pour some of the remaining olive oil into the hot pan, swirling it carefully to coat the entire bottom of the pan. Pour about 1 cup of the batter into the pan. Top the batter with a third of the scallion-parsley mixture, olives, sage, and rosemary.

5. Return the pan to the oven and bake until the top starts getting lightly browned and the sides are lightly crisp, about 10 to 15 minutes. (To make a darker top crust, you may wish to broil the farinata for 1 or 2 minutes at the end of the baking time.) Slide the farinata out of the pan and onto a cutting board. Cut the farinata into 6 pieces. Repeat to make two more farinata. Serve warm.

Pizza Bastarda "Margherita"

Mock Pizza "Margherita"

I NAMED THIS dish *pizza bastarda* (bastardized pizza) for the simple reason that to me, a real pizza has to come from a wood-burning oven that bakes at a very high temperature. As most of us cannot afford to have a brick pizza oven on hand, here is a simple, easy-to-make recipe that will work well in a home oven.

SERVES 4

1 cup warm water (110°F)

2 tsp active dry yeast

¼ tsp honey

3 cups all-purpose flour, or as needed

1 tsp kosher salt or sea salt

2 lb canned San Marzano plum tomatoes, with juices

2 tbsp extra-virgin olive oil, plus as needed

½ cup coarse-chopped fresh basil, plus whole leaves for garnish

Salt and freshly ground black pepper, as needed

1½ lb fresh mozzarella di bufala (fresh cow's milk mozzarella)

Cornmeal for dusting

1. Stir the warm water, yeast, and honey in a mixing bowl until blended, and then let the mixture sit until it becomes foamy, 3 to 5 minutes.

2. Add 2½ cups of flour followed by the salt to the yeast mixture; stir until a heavy dough forms. Turn the dough onto a floured work surface and knead until it is smooth and elastic, about 12 minutes. Continue to dust the dough with the remaining ½ cup of flour to keep it from sticking to your work surface. The dough should be very smooth and elastic, but still soft. Gather the dough into a ball and smooth the outer surface by pinching the underside of the ball together.

3. Grease a clean bowl with some oil. The bowl should be large enough to hold the dough after it has doubled in size. Transfer the dough to the bowl, pinched side down. Cover the dough with a clean, lightly dampened cloth or some plastic wrap. Set the bowl in a warm place and let the dough rise until it doubles in bulk, about 30 minutes.

4. Fold the dough over on itself to press out the air and turn the dough out onto a floured work surface. If you want to make one large pizza, just round the entire ball. To make small pizzas, divide the dough into 2 or 4 equal-sized pieces and make each into a smooth ball by stretching the outer surface and pinching it together at the bottom of the ball. Once the dough balls are rounded, return them to the bowl, cover with a clean cloth, and let the dough rest until it has relaxed enough to stretch out to make the crust, about 20 minutes.

5. While the dough is resting, prepare the topping. Drain the tomatoes of most of their juices; they don't have to be completely dry. Push the tomatoes through a wire mesh sieve or a food mill into a bowl (if your food mill has interchangeable disks, use the one with the largest openings). Stir in 2 tablespoons of olive oil and the chopped basil. Season with salt and pepper and set aside.

6. Slice the mozzarella into ¼-inch-thick slices and spread them on absorbent paper towels to drain, at least 5 minutes.

7. Place a pizza stone in the cold oven and preheat the oven to 500°F.

8. Scatter a little cornmeal on a pizza peel or a flat pan that has no rim and is large enough to accommodate the pizza (a cookie sheet turned upside down works well).

9. Flatten each ball of dough into a flat, round disk. Stretch the dough out to make a thin crust, about ¼ inch thick, and a little thicker on the outer edge. If you like, you can use a rolling pin or you can try tossing and spinning the dough the way you see it done in pizzerias (see note that follows). Slide the crust onto the prepared peel or pan.

10. Put the pizzas together one at a time as follows: Divide the tomato-basil sauce evenly among the number of crusts and spread the sauce evenly over the crust to come within a half inch of the edge. Divide the mozzarella slices in

the same manner, and lay them on top of the sauce, covering the pizzas evenly. Slide the pizzas onto the baking stone and bake the pizzas until the crust is crisp and the outer edges are golden brown, 10 to 12 minutes. (You may need to turn the pizza as it bakes so it cooks evenly.)

11. Slide your peel or pan under the pizza after it has finished baking to get it out of the oven and then put it on a work surface. Put the fresh basil leaves on top of the pizza and drizzle a little more olive oil on top. Cut into slices and serve at once.

||||||||||||||||||||

RECIPE NOTES

You can mix the dough with a mixer using a dough hook as follows: Combine the warm water, yeast, and honey in the bowl of your mixer and let it rest as described above. Add 3 cups of flour and mix with the dough hook on low speed until the flour is blended in completely (scrape the bowl, if necessary, to mix in any flour that might have dropped to the bottom of the bowl), and then increase the speed to medium and continue to mix for 5 to 6 minutes, until the dough forms a ball that "cleans" the side of the bowl.

The stretching action that is the result of tossing your pizza dough in the air gives the crust a crisp texture. First, press the dough into a flat dish and then stretch and turn the dough by turning and stretching the dough in opposite directions with both hands. When the dough is about half the size you want the finished pizza to be, slide your hands under the dough so that it rests on the back of your hands. Toss the dough up in the air, spinning it as you toss, and then catch it on the back of your hands.

ITALIAN BREADS

ITALIANS EAT NEARLY one-half pound of bread every day, compared to only two or three ounces of bread consumed by the typical person in the United States. Perhaps that is because Italians have come to expect not only great variety but also great quality, whether enjoying a *piadini alla romagnola*, *ciabatta*, or *columbo pasquale*. You can find breads made from white wheat flour or whole wheat flour (what Italians refer to as *integrale*), as well as semolina, buckwheat, corn, millet, and even chickpea flours.

The simplest breads are the flatbreads: *pizza*, *piadini*, *focaccia*, and *ciabatta*. These breads are quite simple in and of themselves—usually nothing more than flour, yeast, water, and salt. Some versions include olive oil or milk for a little extra richness. Others depend upon the staggering array of toppings and coatings that Italians enjoy on their bread. "*Pane carasau*" or *carta da musica* (music paper) consists of very thin, crisp circular sheets of dough. Because it keeps well after it is dried, this was the bread eaten by shepherds away from home tending their flocks.

Pane di Altamura is a very crisp, fragrant bread. Its crumb—the soft part of the bread—is the color of straw, and soft to the touch. It keeps for a long time, an essential quality for a bread that was sent along with shepherds who spent weeks at a time in the hills of Alta Murgia. The earliest written document describing the bread of Altamura is Horace's *Satires*, in which the Roman poet recalls that, during a trip to his native land in the spring of A.D. 37, he tasted "the world's most delicious bread—so delicious, in fact, that the discerning traveler stacks up on it for the rest of his journey."

Dark rye flour is used when making breads such as *pan' di segale*. Caraway seeds are often used as a spice in or on the bread.

Hearty, robust breads made into large loaves or even wheels are meant to last a long time, but even these breads begin to stale. Never at a loss for ways to coax flavor and enjoyment out of whatever is at hand, Italians around the country enjoy these breads toasted or grilled and rubbed with olive oil and garlic or a sliced fresh tomato. Bread salad (*panzanella*) and tomato and bread soup (*pappa al pomodoro*) are a few of the ways that bread is brought to the table.

Sweetened breads traditionally served in the spring, like *columbo pasquale* (the dove cake) and *la pastiera* (Neapolitan Easter cake) are made from tender, egg-rich dough, studded with dried fruits and glazed. They mark the end of Lent, and are eagerly anticipated by the faithful after forty days of sacrificing sweets and other treats.

Tigella

Tigella Bread

TIGELLA IS BOTH the name of this popular *focaccia* from Modena, in the Emilia-Romagna region, and the unique tile grills used to bake it. The traditional manner of baking is to press the dough between two very hot rimmed tile disks (*tigelle*), about 3 inches in diameter. The heat held by the tiles bakes the dough into crunchy rounds that you can split and fill with a variety of fillings, from sausage, salami, or cheese, to chocolate or jam. Contemporary tigella grills have electrically heated stone or metal grill surfaces, but an electric sandwich press will work fine.

SERVES 4

1 cake fresh yeast	3½ cups all-purpose flour	3 tbsp olive oil
½ cup whole milk, warmed	½ tsp kosher or sea salt as needed	

1. Dissolve the yeast into the warm milk in a large bowl. Let sit for 1 hour, and then mix in the flour, salt, and oil until the dough is quite soft and comes together. Cover with a clean cloth towel and let rise for about 2 to 3 hours, depending on temperature.

2. Roll the dough out on a floured surface to a thickness of ½ inch. Use a cookie cutter or upside-down glass to cut disks about 2½ to 3 inches in diameter.

3. If you have traditional tigella tiles, preheat them in a 450°F oven until they are very hot, or preheat an electric sandwich press. Put a disk of dough between the two tiles or into the sandwich grill. Bake until the dough is golden on both sides, about 2 to 3 minutes. The tigella is ready to eat now, or it can be split and toasted. Serve them hot.

||||||||||||||||||
RECIPE NOTES

You can make the tigella in a cast iron skillet or on a hot griddle, but it is a little trickier to get them the perfect doneness. Just be prepared to make a few trials before you get it just right.

Piadina alla Romagnola

Cast-Iron Flat Bread with Squaquarone and Prosciutto

LIKE THE TIGELLA, the *piadina* is a popular flat bread found throughout Emilia-Romagna, where it is often eaten fresh-made at a *piadineria*, folded taco-style around various fillings. *Squaquarone* is a soft, round cheese with a mildly tangy flavor made in the region (some of the best regarded cheeses come from Castel San Pietro and Bologna), and is a popular filling for *piadine*.

SERVES 6

3¼ cups all-purpose flour

¼ cup lard or olive oil, at room
    temperature, plus additional

1 tsp kosher or sea salt

½ tsp baking powder

1½ cups warm water (110°F)

2½ cups squaquarone cheese, or a
    combination of cottage and brie

24 thin slices prosciutto

1. Using your hands, a food processor or a mixer, combine the flour, lard or olive oil, salt and baking powder. Add the water slowly and work the dough until it is smooth and elastic. Once the dough is ready to the touch, shape it into a ball and let rest in an oiled bowl, lightly covered, for at least 30 minutes. (If the dough is too wet, turn it out onto a floured work surface and knead a little longer.)

2. Cut the dough into 6 equal pieces and cover each until ready for use. On a lightly floured surface, shape one section at a time into a ball. With a rolling pin, roll out the dough to form an 8-inch disk. Place it on a plate and cover with a cloth. Proceed with the rest of the pieces in the same manner, stacking them on top of each other, making sure they don't stick together.

3. Preheat the oven to 250°F (to keep the finished *piadine* warm while completing the rest). Line an ovenproof dish with a piece of cooking foil.

4. Grease a cast iron pan with a little oil or lard and place over medium-high heat. When the pan is hot, place a disk of dough in the pan. Cook it on one side for 30 seconds, or until lightly browned. Flip the piadina and cook the other side, another 20 to 30 seconds. Transfer the piadina to the foil-lined plate as they are finished and keep warm in the oven. Proceed with the rest of the dough until all of the piadina are cooked.

5. To serve, spread 3 tablespoons of the cheese or other filling over half of each piadina. Top each with 4 slices of prosciutto, fold the piadina in half, and serve.

Focaccia di Patate

Potato Focaccia

WHEN I WAS a chef in a very big restaurant, I always had to have a focaccia on the menu. I used to change the topping every day: olive spread one day, a combination of all kinds of vegetables on another, then perhaps some mozzarella and fresh sliced tomatoes on yet another day.

SERVES 6

¾ lb Idaho potatoes

2½ cups warm water (110°F)

1¼ tsp dry yeast

½ tsp sugar

2½ cups bread flour

1 tbsp kosher salt or sea salt

½ cup extra-virgin olive oil, plus
  more for oiling the pan

¾ lb canned crushed tomatoes

½ cup coarse chopped fresh basil

Dried oregano as needed

1. Put the potatoes in a deep pot and add enough cold water to cover them by about 1 inch. Add salt to taste and bring to a boil over high heat. Reduce the heat enough to make the water simmer gently and cook the potatoes until they are tender enough to pierce easily with the tip of a paring knife, about 15 to 20 minutes (longer if your potatoes are very large). Remove the potatoes and let them cool just until you can handle them; they should be as hot as possible. (The potatoes can be left whole; they will be mashed into a puree as you mix the dough.)

2. Stir the water, yeast, and sugar together in a mixing bowl until blended, then let the mixture sit until it becomes foamy, 3 to 5 minutes.

3. Combine the warm potatoes with 2 cups of the flour in a large mixing bowl. (You can do this in a stand mixer, but I prefer to mix it by hand. It is a very soft dough, so it isn't hard to mix with a wooden spoon.) Once you've blended in the flour, add the salt and mix it in. Gradually add the yeast-water mixture and the olive oil and mix until it is very smooth and elastic, but still very wet and soft; it should still hold together. (You may need to add a bit more flour if the day is humid.) Place the dough in a large, lightly oiled bowl and cover it with a clean, lightly dampened cloth or some plastic wrap. Set the bowl in a warm place and let the dough rise until it doubles in bulk, about 1 hour.

4. Preheat the oven to 450°F. Generously oil two 9-inch round pans (cake pans will work). Drop the dough into the pans and spread it out to the edges. Spoon half of the tomatoes, basil, and oregano on top of each round of dough and let it rise again, about 20 minutes. Using your fingers, gently dimple the surface of the foccacias and bake until the dough is baked through and the edges are browned, about 20 minutes. Cut into wedges and serve warm.

Focaccia di Recco allo Stracchino con Pomodoro

Focaccia with Stracchino and Tomato

THIS FOCACCIA IS a specialty of Recco, a tiny coastal town near Genoa. *Stracchino* is a soft, almost spreadable cheese similar to Brie, but without a rind. You can substitute mascarpone or another cheese with a similar texture. If you wish, add some procsiutto to the focaccia before you bake it.

SERVES 6

3½ cups bread flour

5 tbsp extra-virgin olive oil, plus as needed for oiling pan

½ cup warm water (110°F), or as needed

1 tsp kosher or sea salt, as needed

1 lb stracchino cheese, or any cheese similar to brie, sliced

2 fresh tomatoes, thinly sliced

1. Mix the flour with the oil. Slowly add the water and salt, mixing until well combined. Allow the dough to rest for at least 30 minutes.

2. Liberally sprinkle a work surface with flour. Using a rolling pin, roll half of the dough out very thin. (The dough may be sticky, so make sure the rolling pin is always well floured.)

3. Oil an 11 × 16 inch baking sheet and place the dough on it, spreading it as thin as possible onto the pan. Top with a layer of sliced cheese.

4. Preheat the oven to 400°F. (Note: A convection oven works well for this recipe.)

5. Roll out the remaining dough in the same way and lay it over the cheese. Pinch together the entire border to seal it well and prevent the cheese from oozing out. Poke the top with a fork, brush with a little oil and water, and bake for about 10 minutes. Make sure you keep an eye on the focaccia while it is baking because the dough is very thin and can burn quickly. Once lightly browned, remove and let rest for 3 to 5 minutes so the cheese can solidify somewhat. Place the tomato slices on top, cut, and serve while still warm.

FOCACCIA

The word *focaccia* refers to several varieties of flat, yeast-raised breads found in Italian cuisine. The bread was referred to in Roman times as *panis focacius*, and was cooked on the hearth or under the ashes of the fire. The dough for a focaccia is related to that used for pizza, and is rolled out and topped with various seasonings or additions, then baked. The surface of a focaccia is often dimpled in several places with a finger or utensil, maximizing the area of crust, as well as providing little pockets where oil and flavorings can accumulate. Focaccia loaves freeze well, and are excellent reheated. There are numerous regional variations on the basic recipe, from savory to sweet, and focaccia has become quite well-known outside of Italy. It is a popular choice as a sandwich bread, especially for *panini*.

"PIZZA" DI SPAGHETTI

SPAGHETTI PIZZA

USE A GOOD MOZZARELLA in this dish such as a mozzarella *fiordilatte*—a good fresh mozzarella made from cow's milk. The pasta should be firm (*al dente*), since you will finish cooking it in the oven. Don't worry too much because the point of this recipe is that it is the perfect way to use up the leftover spaghetti from the night before. You'll need about 4 or 5 cups of cooked pasta to make 6 servings.

SERVES 6

6 ounces dry spaghetti

¼ cup extra-virgin olive oil, as needed

8 oz mozzarella, *fior di latte* if possible

18 black olives, any good quality

6 oil-packed anchovies

8 oz peeled San Marzano tomatoes, crushed by hand to
　　break into pieces

2 tsp Sicilian dry oregano

Salt and freshly ground black pepper, as needed

1. Preheat the oven to 350°F.
2. Cook the spaghetti in plenty of salted water until very *al dente*. Drain well, sprinkle with half of the olive oil, and toss slightly. Place the spaghetti into small casserole dishes for individual servings or in two 8-inch casseroles that have been lightly oiled. Make sure the spaghetti is flat by lightly pressing it into an even layer.

3. Cut the mozzarella into ¼-inch-thick slices. Pit the olives and then slice them thin.

4. Cover the top of the spaghetti with the mozzarella slices. Divide the anchovies between the casseroles, and then spread the crushed tomatoes on top followed by the olives, oregano, salt, and pepper. Drizzle with the remaining olive oil.

5. Bake for about 20 minutes until the mozzarella has completely melted. Serve very hot.

> *"Chi mangia bene, vive bene."*

Who eats well, lives well.

— ITALIAN PROVERB

HOLIDAYS AND FOOD

HOLIDAYS ARE WHEN Italian culinary artistry is at its best. I love every stage—from the pre-planning rituals to the big event. The menu is elaborated and finalized with the help of other family members. The shopping is done at least a day before, but not more than a week in advance to make sure that everything is as fresh as possible. All the deals to strike with the vendors. Then, getting the house ready. Relatives gathering in the kitchen, finishing up the preparations. Smells familiar and nostalgic traveling all over the house and permeating your clothes. Setting out the best linens, china, and flatware. Stressing about timing. And finally watching as what seemed like an impossible and endless ritual comes to an end with the last kiss goodbye.

Sunday is one of our favorite "holidays," with the advantage that it comes along every week! On that day everyone seems to sleep in, as it is the only day of the week when children aren't in school. Everyone sleeps in except for the chef, that is, who is up early and in the kitchen preparing dishes for the two meals of the day. Sunday is the only day of the week when Italians typically enjoy a big breakfast; otherwise we aren't big on that meal. On Sundays it's a necessity because lunch and dinner are combined into one extended meal that doesn't start until the middle of the afternoon, making it a definite stretch to last until dinner begins unless you've had a more substantial breakfast.

Sunday is also the day that all the regional soccer games are played.

The normal starting time is 3:00 p.m. and that is the time that the table is set. Since the game of soccer is by far the most popular one in Italy, homes are usually full of friends, family, and neighbors by then. The radios and the televisions are on and the volume is loud. The streets are empty, and for the next two hours everyone is occupied with cheering and screaming for their favorite team.

Sunday dinner is served in multiple courses, with long pauses between courses. Usually, the first course is appreciated through the first half-time of the game. Right after that, the entrée is served accompanied by *contorni* (vegetables). This ritual usually lasts until 7 or 8 in the evening.

The signature Sunday dish is definitely the *ragu*. It is a tomato sauce that gets started early in the morning with its main ingredients of fresh tomato, condiments, seasonings, and a large piece of meat that cooks along with the tomato sauce, releasing plenty of flavor and a bit of fat into the sauce itself. The cooking time seems endless and the flame is always low. Northern Italians feel that fresh pasta is the best to pair with their ragu, but Southern Italians prefer dry pasta.

By the end of the game the mood might be happy or sad, depending on the score. But, whatever the mood there is still the final course to enjoy. For our family this was either fried fish accompanied by a salad, or a fritto misto (a mixed fry), a combination of potato croquettes, fried zucchini, cauliflower, artichoke, and other fresh vegetables.

Since dessert is not our strong point, we, like many other Italians, have a cheese course at the table to end the meal. On Sundays, though, it is our ritual to buy sweets from our local pastry shop. After that, we end the day with a game of tombola, the Italian version of bingo.

Christmas celebrations, and the foods that go along with them, are without doubt the most important of the Italian culinary calendar. Our most important night is the Vigilia, Christmas Eve. Dinner is served late in the evening and fish is the theme, giving this meal its name: the Celebration of the Seven Fishes.

Why seven fishes? Many claim that seven is for the number of the sacraments in the Roman Catholic faith and that each fish represents one sacrament. Each fish (or sacrament) must be prepared in a different method. Others claim that seven is the number of the days of the week and that each fish represents a specific day. Another theory is that the number signifies the Seven Wonders of the World. And, finally, the number of fish may also stand for the seven winds in Italy.

Whichever version of the story you prefer, the meal always consists of an elaborate array of at least seven fish dishes featuring clams, cod, snapper, eel, squid, shrimp, scallops, mussels, and more. One of the traditional accompaniments to this meal is known as insalata di rinforzo (strength salad), a cauliflower salad with anchovies, capers, hot peppers, and olives dressed with vinegar.

Despite the seven-course meal served on Christmas Eve, the meal is not so filling that a complete meal cannot be enjoyed on Christmas Day. There are some traditions to observe for this meal as well. It usually starts with the minestra maritata (wedding soup) made from a variety of vegetables including kale, escarole, broccoletti, celery, and carrots. The soup is finished with shredded meats and cheese.

The purpose of this soup is to cleanse you following the fish ritual from the day before. This prepares you for the next course of the Christmas feast. In some regions you might enjoy a turkey, while in others pork, lamb, or beef is preferred. Even the accompaniments served this day are richer than those served the previous day.

Dessert on Christmas Day is a nearly endless parade that features many ancient sweets traditional to the day. Struffoli is one of the most popular ones. Little fritters are mixed with honey and topped with candied fruits and sugar colored balls. Roccoco is an almond paste confection shaped like a flat bagel that is ready to serve when it's extremely hard. (Some people I know have broken a tooth or two in the process of attempting to eat them!)

Panettone is a cake made from a sweet bread dough filled with candied fruits and raisins, and they are found everywhere in Italy to serve on Christmas. There is a legend that claims that a baker by the name of Toni created this dessert and gave it its name: panettone, or *pane di Toni*—Toni's bread. As the story goes, he woke up too late to make the dessert the correct way, so he simply mixed all the ingredients for the dough together at once and baked it. Luckily for everyone, the results were delicious.

Easter is another holiday where religion and the culinary arts meet at the table. Foods that symbolize rebirth and resurrection are made with an abundance of eggs, butter, and sugar. The shapes and colors of the foods are all part of the celebration. Pretzels, for example, were originally Easter food; the shape thought to resemble arms crossed in prayer.

Air-cured meats are enjoyed in a bountiful antipasto known as *affettato*, consisting of various *salami, sopressata, capicollo* with *ricotta salata* (a firm version of ricotta that is salted) and hard-boiled eggs, a recurrent symbol of the Easter season that shows up in several dishes.

At Easter time a savory tart called *tortano* is made. It is a tart made with a dough similar to peasant bread, and stuffed with a mixture of diced *salami, mortadella, prosciutto*, and a variety of cubed cheeses. The completed tart is garnished with hard-boiled eggs, too.

Italians lay claim to the invention of chocolate eggs. Ours are generally bigger than the usual version and each one carries a surprise gift inside.

A very ancient and very unusual dessert (but one that has been declining in popularity over the past few decades for obvious reasons) is *sanguinaccio*, a chocolate sauce that is mixed with pork blood.

There are special holidays and occasions throughout the year. Festivals and religious holidays all seem to have their own special food. At New Year's Eve, the *cenone* (big dinner) is celebrated. On this occasion we enjoy *cotechino* or *zampone* (a fresh pork sausage and stuffed pig's trotters respectively), served with a spoonful with lentils. Tradition dictates that if you count the lentils and make the same number of wishes as you have lentils, they will all come true in the New Year.

During Carnival in Italy (the time just before Ash Wednesday and the start of Lent) *lasagna* is appreciated. Father's Day is celebrated on March 19 in Italy; it is also the feast day of San Giuseppe (Saint Joseph). *Zeppole* (fried doughnuts rolled in sugar) are the signature dish on that occasion.

CHAPTER THREE

POLENTA, RISO E PASTA

Polenta, Rice, and Pasta

POLENTA SPORCACCIONA

"NAUGHTY" POLENTA

THE OWNER OF the Agriturismo Riva Grande, a tiny three-room *pensione* in Molvena, a village close to where I grew up, keeps a part of her fields strictly free of any pesticides or other chemicals to grow corn for polenta. You can arrange in advance to have dinner there, and she will make you one of the best meals imaginable. She grinds the corn for her polenta right there with a small grinder into her copper cauldron. A few hours later you'll have the best polenta you have ever tasted. She is such a purist in everything she does, from making salami to even making her own wines. Unbelievable!

In different areas of Italy, especially in the north, you will find every conceivable addition to polenta, including spareribs, cabbage, vegetables, beans, little pieces of fried lard, and so on. Use a good-quality polenta, coarse, if possible, and organic if you can find it. The polenta is considered "naughty" because of the amount of butter floating on the top—it is up to you to decide how naughty you like your polenta.

SERVES 6

6 cups water, plus as needed to adjust consistency

2 tbsp kosher salt, or as needed

1½ cups yellow polenta

1 cup diced Maccagno or Fontina cheese

⅓ cup lightly browned butter, or extra-virgin olive oil

1. In a heavy-bottomed pot, bring the water to a boil. Add the salt and slowly add the polenta, using a whisk to mix and break up any clumps. Once the polenta starts getting dense, switch to a sturdy wooden spoon and keep on stirring.

2. Cook very slowly over low heat for 40 minutes, continuing to stir every 4 or 5 minutes. Once the polenta is cooked (it shouldn't be too stiff), stir in the cheese and serve in bowl.

3. Just before bringing the dish to the table, pour the lightly browned butter on top or drizzle with some good olive oil.

||||||||||||||||||

RECIPE NOTES

Try adding a few fresh sage leaves and a very thin slice of onion to the pan while the butter melts for additional flavor. As soon as it is a nice brown, usually a minute or two, pour it into a dish to stop the cooking and keep it from taking on a bitter flavor.

Other cheeses that can be used are Bitto or Casera, but Taleggio or Zola will work well also.

As an alternate method for serving the polenta, pour half of the cooked polenta into an ovenproof casserole, spread half of the cheese on top, and then top with the remaining polenta and cheese. Drizzle with the brown butter and bake the polenta in the oven at 350°F for 12 to 15 minutes or just until the cheese is hot and melted. You could add a layer of cooked sausage in between the polenta layers for a complete meal.

Risotto di Escarola con Provolone Affumicato

Risotto with Escarole and Smoked Provolone

IN ITALY WE say *e' un peccato mortale* (it's a mortal sin or a blasphemy) to use the wrong pot to cook risotto. You need a deep saucepan (2-quart for about 1½ cups of rice, which will give you about 4 cups of risotto, including the garnish). Absolutely avoid using a sauté pan or skillet—you will find that the liquid evaporates too quickly before the rice has a chance to absorb it.

There are many myths about stirring the rice. My opinion is that you don't need to keep on stirring the rice constantly, especially during the first 10 minutes. Just make sure to keep the rice wet at all times during the first stage of cooking, and gently stir it every few minutes during the simmering stage to make sure the rice doesn't stick on the bottom of the pan and stays uniformly wet at all times.

There is also strong sentiment regarding the proper way to serve risotto. Serving risotto in a bowl instead of on a flat plate is another *peccato mortale*. You are supposed to start eating your risotto beginning from the outside edge of the plate, so that the rice has time to cool slightly as you eat it, enabling you to really enjoy the flavor.

A good broth is one of the keys to a successful risotto, and for the best results, it should be boiling hot when you add it to the rice in the pan. There are also differences in the cooking qualities of different types of rice, and the results you get from this recipe will vary depending upon the rice you use. Once you find a good quality brand of rice that you like, stick with it for the most consistent results.

SERVES 4

½ cup minced onion	2 cups packed escarole, washed and coarsely cut	½ cup grated Parmigiano-Reggiano cheese, or as needed
2 tbsp olive oil, butter or a combination of both	5 cups beef, chicken, or vegetable broth	¼ cup chopped fresh parsley
1½ cups superfino rice (Arborio, Carnaroli, or Vialone Nano)	4 tbsp unsalted butter, room temperature	½ cup small-dice smoked provolone
½ cup dry white wine		Salt and freshly ground black pepper, as needed

1. In a deep saucepan over medium heat, cook the onion with the oil or butter or a combination of both until it is soft but not browned. Add the rice and stir it, so that the rice gets well coated with the fat. Once the rice is uniformly hot, add the wine and the escarole. Let the wine cook until it almost completely evaporates. Slowly start adding 4 cups of the broth (make sure the liquid is boiling hot) in 3 equal parts, about 1⅓ cups at a time, making sure the rice absorbs all of the liquid from each addition before you add the next. *(recipe continues on next page)*

2. After about 12 to 13 minutes of simmering, add the remaining cup of broth a little at a time making sure that, once it is ready, the risotto is not too wet. You can always add more liquid if needed, but if you add too much, it is difficult to adjust the consistency without overcooking the rice. Remember, the risotto is supposed to be served *al dente*, not overcooked or mushy.

3. Turn the heat off and remove the pan from the stove. Add the butter and mix vigorously. Then add the parmesan cheese and parsley. Just before you are ready to serve the risotto, add the smoked cheese and stir until cheese is almost melted. Adjust the seasoning with salt and pepper and serve immediately. Make sure the rice is *all'onda* (wavelike) and not stiff.

Farrotto con Guanciale, Pomodorini, Timo e Pecorino

Farro "Risotto-style" with Guanciale, Small Tomatoes, Thyme, and Aged Pecorino

THIS IS DEFINITELY a winter dish, with its characteristically chewy texture and nutty flavor. Follow the same rules as if you were making a risotto. Give yourself more time, however, because the farro will require more time to cook—about twice as long as risotto, 30 to 35 minutes.

SERVES 6

½ cup minced onion

¼ cup small-dice celery, peeled before dicing

1 tbsp extra-virgin olive oil, plus additional 1½ tsp

½ cup medium-dice guanciale or pancetta

1¼ cups whole grain farro

¾ cup red wine, preferably Chianti or similar

2 tbsp fresh thyme, leaves only

5 cups beef, chicken or vegetable broth

1 cup each cherry, grape, and pear tomatoes, halved if they are large, to make a total of 3 cups

¾ cup grated aged Tuscan pecorino cheese

Salt and freshly ground black pepper, as needed

1. In a proper casserole over medium heat, sweat the onion and the celery in 1 tablespoon of the oil until translucent, about 4 minutes. Add the guanciale or pancetta, and keep cooking at low heat until the guanciale or pancetta is well rendered, about 3 minutes.

2. Add the farro and stir so that the farro gets well coated with the fat. Once the farro is uniformly hot, about 2 minutes, add the wine and cook until it evaporates, about 6 minutes. Mix in 1 tablespoon of the fresh thyme and then pour in 2½ cups of the broth. Bring the farro to a gentle simmer over low heat, making sure to stir it every few minutes.

3. After about 12 to 15 minutes of simmering, add half of the tomatoes and the remaining broth and keep simmering for another 15 minutes. Once the farro is cooked, remove it from

the heat, making sure at this point the farro is not too liquid. If it is too soupy, continue cooking, so it can absorb the excess liquid. Whole grain farro is more forgiving than risotto because it is less likely to overcook.

4. Add the remaining tomatoes, the cheese, and the remaining thyme. Mix vigorously so that you will create a creamy *farrotto*. Adjust the seasoning with salt and pepper as needed. Just before serving incorporate 1½ teaspoons of good

quality extra-virgin olive oil, some additional freshly ground pepper, and serve immediately.

|||||||||||||||
RECIPE NOTES

Leftover *farrotto* can be used to make a quick snack. Add a large beaten egg, some bread crumbs if you need to firm up the consistency (the mixture should hold together when pressed into a cake), and whatever vegetables you have—cooked peas, chopped cooked artichokes, cooked zucchini, etc. Form into patties, pan fry in olive oil, and serve warm or hot.

Fregola e Arselle alla Sarda

Sardinian Couscous with Tiny Clams

YOU CAN USE mussels for this recipe as well, or a combination of mussels and clams. The clams must be small—the smaller the better. Serve with a good Sardinian wine such as Nugarus or Vermentino.

SERVES 4

2 qt fish broth, very light, or vegetable broth

½ lb fregola sarda (Sardinian couscous)

½ cup extra-virgin olive oil

4 garlic cloves, crushed

¼ cup roughly chopped parsley

½ cup chopped basil

¼ cup chopped sun-dried tomatoes

1 lb peeled crushed tomatoes

Salt and freshly ground black pepper, as needed

2 lb baby clams, cleaned

2 tsp chopped fresh oregano

1. In a large saucepan, bring the broth to a boil, add the fregola, and let simmer for about 10 minutes over low heat, making sure it doesn't stick together.

2. While the fregola is cooking, in a separate pan over medium heat, warm ⅓ cup of the oil with the garlic, half of the parsley, half of the basil, and the sun-dried tomatoes. Add the peeled crushed tomatoes, season with salt and

pepper as needed, and let cook for 5 to 8 minutes. Add the baby clams and let them cook until they are just open, about 8 minutes.

3. Once the clams have opened, add the tomato-clam mixture to the fregola, and finish cooking for another 2 to 3 minutes. When ready to serve, add the remaining parsley, basil, and oregano, and drizzle with some good olive oil. Serve very hot.

MAKING FRESH PASTA BY HAND

DECIDING ON THE amount of pasta to cook for each person depends on how the dish will be served. A light first course in a meal with several courses—the way pasta is served at most Italian tables—calls for less pasta than a hearty main-dish pasta served with only a salad. A general guideline for a first course calls for about 4 ounces of fresh pasta or 2 ounces dried pasta per person.

Dried pastas are made from hard-wheat flours, such as semolina, which produce a stiff dough that is difficult to knead or roll by hand. Dried pastas of excellent quality in a variety of shapes, sizes, colors, and flavors are widely available. Since they keep almost indefinitely in a cool, dry, dark cupboard, you can always have some on hand.

Fresh pasta is made from flour, eggs, and salt. Sometimes, you may add a bit of oil or water for pliability, or additional ingredients to add flavor or color—spices, vegetable purees, or citrus zest. While you can buy fresh pasta, it is not difficult to make your own. The only tools you need are a flat work surface, your hands, a fork, and a rolling pin.

Ingredients for fresh pasta

All-purpose flour works well for making fresh pasta at home. Eggs provide moisture, flavor, and structure. (Dried pasta sometimes includes eggs, but water is typically the only liquid used.) Some fresh pasta recipes also call for a small amount of water or oil to make the dough tender and pliable. Salt develops flavor in the dough. You can substitute a quantity of whole-wheat, semolina, cornmeal, buckwheat, rye, or chickpea flour for all-purpose flour to give your pasta a unique flavor and texture. Ingredients such as spinach or saffron also may be added for flavor and color.

Mixing ingredients

For small batches, pasta dough can be efficiently mixed by hand. Combine the flour and salt in a bowl and make a well in the center. Place the eggs, flavoring ingredients, and oil in the well. Using a fork and working as rapidly as possible, incorporate the flour into the liquid ingredients little by little working from the outside toward the center, until a shaggy mass forms. As the dough is mixed, adjust the consistency with additional flour or a few drops of water to compensate for the natural variations in ingredients, humidity, temperature, or the addition of either dry or moist flavoring ingredients.

Kneading

Once the dough is mixed, turn it out onto a floured surface and knead until its texture becomes smooth and elastic. Use the heels of your hands to push the dough away from you, and then reverse the motion, folding the dough over on itself toward you. Give the dough a quarter turn periodically so that it is evenly kneaded. Kneading by hand generally takes 10 to 12 minutes. Do not rush the kneading process or the texture of the finished pasta will suffer. Properly kneaded dough is uniform in texture and no longer tacky to the touch. Divide the dough into balls about the size of an orange, place in a bowl, and cover loosely with a cotton towel. Allow the dough to rest at room temperature for at least 30 minutes. This will relax the dough and make it easier to roll out.

Rolling and cutting

Use a straight wooden rolling pin to roll out pasta dough. Lightly flour a work surface. Use just enough flour to prevent the dough from sticking. Too much flour will cause the pasta to be dry. Work with one ball of dough at a time. Keep the remaining dough covered to prevent it from drying out. Flatten the dough by pressing it into a disk, and then begin rolling. Try to keep the dough's thickness even as you work. Turn the dough to keep it from sticking and lightly flour the rolling pin and the work surface if necessary.

When the dough is as thin as you want it, you can cut it into sheets. After the dough is cut into sheets, it can be cut into long, flat, ribbon shapes like papardelle, linguini, or fettucini. Roll a sheet of pasta dough up into a cylinder and make crosswise cuts of the desired width: very wide for papardelle to very narrow for linguini. These sheets can also be cut into squares or circles to fill and fold into tortellini or ravioli, as described below.

MAKING FRESH PASTA BY MACHINE

Large batches of pasta dough are easier to make with a food processor or stand mixer. To mix in a food processor, fit the machine with the metal blade and combine all the ingredients in its work bowl. Process just until the dough is blended into a coarse meal that forms a ball when gathered. Do not overprocess. Remove the dough, transfer to a lightly floured work surface, and knead by hand as described above.

To use a stand mixer, fit it with the dough hook attachment to combine all the ingredients, and then mix at low speed for 3 to 4 minutes, until the dough is just moistened. Increase the speed to medium and knead the dough another 3 minutes, until the dough forms a smooth ball that pulls cleanly away from the sides of the bowl.

Rolling the dough in a pasta machine

Gather the dough into a ball, cover, and allow to relax at room temperature for at least 30 minutes. Letting the dough relax allows it to be rolled into thin sheets more easily. Cut off a piece of dough and flatten it. The amount will vary according to the width of your pasta ma-

chine. Cover the remaining dough to keep it from drying. Set the rollers to the widest opening, fold the dough in thirds, and guide the flattened dough through the machine as you turn the handle. Roll the dough to form a long, wide strip. Pass the dough through the widest setting 2 or 3 times, folding the dough in thirds each time.

Lightly flour the dough strip to prevent sticking. Set the rollers to the next thinnest opening and run the dough through the rollers again without folding. Repeat, narrowing the setting, lightly dusting the dough with flour each time, and passing the dough through the rollers twice on each setting, until it reaches the desired thinness—the second-to-last setting for most pastas, or the thinnest setting for lasagna.

Cutting and drying the dough

Cut each rolled sheet of dough into shorter lengths, about 1 foot long, for easier handling. For best results—cleaner cuts and no sticking—let the pasta sheets dry slightly until the surface is leathery to the touch. This is especially important for cutting shapes by hand, but machine cutting is also easier with slightly dried pasta. Feed the dough through the desired cutting attachment. If you are not cooking the pasta immediately, you can dry it for storage. Spread small shapes in a single layer on a clean, dry towel or baking sheet. Gather long pasta into loose nests, arrange them on a clean baking sheet with plenty of space between each one, and let the pasta dry completely in a cool, dry place before placing in an airtight container. Store in the refrigerator for up to 2 days.

MAKING STUFFED PASTA

When making stuffed pastas, you can add a small amount of vegetable oil to the dough to help it stick together better when sealed around a filling. Roll the pasta out to the thinnest setting on a pasta machine. While rolling and filling one portion of the dough, keep the rest tightly wrapped in plastic wrap to make sure it stays moist and pliable. Cut and fill the sheets as soon as possible after they are rolled. As they dry, they become more difficult to seal properly.

Forming ravioli

Lightly flour a clean, dry work surface and lay down a thinly rolled pasta sheet. Use a round cookie cutter to cut out as many rounds as possible, or use a sharp knife to cut squares.

Using a teaspoon or a pastry bag, place or pipe a small amount of the filling in the center of each circle or square. The amount of filling will vary depending on the size of the pasta round or square. Lightly moisten the edges of the pasta round or square with a pastry brush dipped in cool water. Top each with another pasta round or square and press firmly with your fingertips to seal. Use the tines of a fork to crimp the edges together. Refrigerate the finished ravioli while you roll out, cut, and fill the remaining pasta dough.

Forming tortellini

Lightly flour a clean, dry work surface and lay down a thinly rolled pasta sheet. Use a round cookie cutter to cut out as many rounds as possible, or use a sharp knife to cut squares. Using a teaspoon or a pastry bag, place or pipe a small amount of the filling in the center of each circle or square. The amount of filling will vary depending on the size of the pasta round or square. Lightly moisten the edges of the pasta round or square with a pastry brush dipped in cool water, fold in half to make a half-moon or triangle, and press firmly to seal with your fingertips. To shape the tortellini, wrap the half circle or triangle around the tip of your forefinger, pull the 2 corners together to overlap and pinch them firmly to seal.

PREPARING PASTA

A large pot that is taller than it is wide is best for boiling most pastas. Stuffed pastas such as raviolis, however, are best cooked in wide, shallow pans that allow for easier removal.

Fill the pot with plenty of water and bring the water to a rolling boil. For every pound of pasta, allow about 1 gallon of water. Add 2 tablespoons of salt per gallon of water for the best-tasting finished dish. The water should taste noticeably salty, like seawater.

Cooking pasta

Once the water comes to a full boil, add the pasta all at once. Long strands should be submerged gently as they soften. Stir the pasta a few times to separate the strands or shapes, then cook until al dente—that is, tender but still offering resistance to the bite. Fresh pasta cooks rapidly, often taking less than 1 minute. Dried pasta requires 5 to 12 minutes or even longer, depending on the size and shape. When it is ready, pour the pasta into a colander and toss well to drain away as much water as possible.

Saucing pasta

Sauces are customarily paired with pasta shapes that complement both their texture and flavor. Hearty sauces require sturdier shapes, such as bucatoni, to stand up to their weight, while smooth sauces, such as pesto, benefit from thinner strands that are easily coated. The delicate flavor of fresh pasta is best matched with a simple sauce based on oil, cream, or butter. Stuffed pastas also call for light sauces, as their fillings provide flavor and moisture of their own. See the chart on the following page for guidance in matching sauces to pasta shapes.

Pasta doesn't always demand a traditional simmered sauce. Keep a chunk of fresh Parmesan cheese, some olive oil, and garlic on hand

and you can whip up dinner in less time than it takes to run out for a pizza. With some key pantry staples in your inventory—sun-dried tomatoes, canned tomatoes, olives, ca-pers, dried mushrooms, anchovies, and arti-choke hearts, to name a few—you can pre-pare or devise countless delicious pasta sauces. Stock your refrigerator and freezer with ingre-dients like eggs, prosciutto, pancetta, chorizo or other cured sausage, heavy cream, butter, pesto, fresh herbs, and vegetables for great im-promptu pasta meals.

Pairing shapes and sauces

TYPE	EXAMPLES	SAUCE SUGGESTIONS
Long, thin strands	Capellini, spaghetti, linguine, vermicelli, bucatini bavette, macheroni alla chitarra	Olive oil or tomato sauces
Long, wide ribbons	Fettuccine, tagliatelle, pappardelle, trenette, lasagnette	Smooth, light butter- or cream-based sauces
Tubes	Penne, rigatoni, macaroni, bucatoni, mostaccioli, tortiglioni, ziti	Chunky sauces with meat and vegetables
Pockets	Shells, orecchiette	Chunky sauces with meat and vegetables
Twists	Fusilli, rotini, gemelli	Slightly chunky meat or vegetable sauces
Frilled	Radiatore, farfalle, farfallini, fusilli, gigli, campanelle, cresti di gallo	Smooth sauces with vegetables
Small	Orzo, ditali, ditalini, stelline	Butter, herbs
Stuffed	Ravioli, tortellini, cappelletti, manicotti, agnolotti, rotolo, cannelloni	Butter, broth, pesto, grated cheese

PASTA AL UOVO

FRESH EGG PASTA

YOU CAN READ many legends and myths concerning who made the "original" pasta, but with the credit going to the Etruscans, the Chinese, and the Greeks, as well as the Italians. While Italians may or may not have created the dish, they have certainly carried it around the world. When fresh egg pasta first came on the U.S. culinary scene in the 1980s, there was an immediate rush by home cooks to try their hand and pasta machines became a coveted kitchen tool. For the best results, roll the dough with a machine, but cut it by hand.

MAKES 1¼ POUNDS OF FRESH PASTA. SERVES 6 AS AN APPETIZER OR 4 AS AN ENTRÉE

1 lb all-purpose flour

4 large eggs

1 tbsp olive oil

Salt

1. Mound the flour on a clean surface. Create a well in the center and place the eggs with the oil in the center. Using a fork, whisk the eggs and slowly start dragging the flour into the egg mixture. Help hold the walls of flour in place with your hand so the egg mixture doesn't run out.

2. Once the flour is evenly moistened, knead well until all the ingredients are well combined and the dough seems smooth and elastic. Wrap the dough in plastic wrap or place it in a covered bowl and let it rest for at least 30 minutes.

3. Using a pasta roller, or by hand with a rolling pin, flatten the pasta, making sure you keep dusting your work surface with more flour at each turn to keep the pasta from sticking. Roll out the pasta to make an 8- × 12-inch rectangle, about ⅛ inch thick.

4. Cut the pasta into 12-inch long strips. At this stage, the pasta can be cut into shapes for filling, or use a knife or the pasta machine cutter to cut the pasta into spaghetti or other width. Place the cut pasta on parchment paper until ready to use. The pasta can also be frozen for several weeks.

Pasta Integrale

Whole Wheat Pasta

IF YOU WANT to make your own whole wheat pasta, the traditional shape used is for *bigoli*, but if you don't have a *bigolaro* or *torchio* (the utensil used to make *bigoli*), make spaghetti instead—just make it a little thicker than usual.

MAKES 1¼ POUNDS OF FRESH PASTA. SERVES 6 AS AN APPETIZER OR 4 AS AN ENTRÉE

1 cup whole wheat flour

2 cups durum flour, plus more for dusting.

3 large eggs

1 tbsp olive oil

Water as needed

1. Combine the flours and mound on a clean surface. Create a well in the center and add the eggs and oil in the center. Using a fork, whisk the eggs and slowly start dragging the flour into the egg mixture. Help hold the walls of flour in place with your hand so the egg mixture doesn't run out.

2. Once the flour is evenly moistened, knead well until all the ingredients are well combined and the dough seems smooth and elastic. Wrap the dough in plastic wrap or place it in a covered bowl and let it rest for at least 30 minutes.

3. Using a pasta roller or by hand with a rolling pin, flatten the pasta making sure you keep dusting your work surface with more flour at each turn to keep the pasta from sticking. Roll out the pasta to make an 8- × 12-inch rectangle, about ⅛ inch thick.

4. Cut the pasta into 12-inch long strips. At this stage, the pasta can be cut into shapes for filling, or use a knife or the pasta machine cutter to cut the pasta into spaghetti or other width. Place the cut pasta on parchment paper until ready to use. The pasta can also be frozen for several weeks.

Salsa al Pomodoro Veloce

Quick Tomato Sauce

THIS IS JUST one interpretation of the many tomato sauce recipes to be found throughout Italy. It is very easy to make, and when fresh, ripe plum (Roma) tomatoes are available, they are the ideal choice to use in this recipe. If you can't find a source of good-quality ripe tomatoes, use good-quality canned ones instead. There are many excellent Italian canned tomato products available, and trust me, they are a much better choice than using watery, flavorless, out-of-season fresh tomatoes.

MAKES 1 QUART

½ cup extra-virgin olive oil

½ cup minced red onions

½ tsp minced garlic

3 lb canned Italian plum tomatoes, drained and roughly chopped

Salt and freshly ground black pepper, as needed

½ cup fresh basil, torn into small pieces

1. In a 3-quart saucepan, heat the olive oil over medium-low heat. Add the onion and sauté until soft, about 6 minutes. Add the garlic and, after it releases a good aroma, about 1 minute, add the tomatoes. Simmer over low heat until the tomatoes are very soft, about 20 minutes. Turn off the heat and allow the sauce to cool for 15 minutes.

2. Pass the sauce through a food mill fitted with the insert with the largest holes. (If you like your tomato sauce coarse, just use a whisk to break the biggest pieces.) Add salt and pepper to taste and stir in the basil. Heat over low heat and combine with cooked pasta, or set aside for later use.

IIIIIIIIIIIIIIIII
RECIPE NOTES

All the conflicting instructions you may have heard about tomato sauce (use sugar, never add sugar, add wine, never add wine, etc.) are part of our Italian tradition. Don't let this get in the way and confuse you about how to make a good sauce. Remember, it is just tomato sauce—don't get yourself too crazy over "right" and "wrong." Just keep on trying until you find a combination of ingredients that suits your palate.

If the tomatoes are very acid, you may want to add a bit of celery and carrot to the base along with the onion to cut down the acidity.

Ragu di Luganica con Finocchio

Luganica Ragù with Fresh Fennel

THIS IS ONE of the thousands recipes you will find under the general heading of either ragu or sauce Bolognese. You will find recipes that use different vegetables as the base, different fats, different herbs, and so forth. Some may have chicken liver, prosciutto, or mortadella. You can find one you like and stick with it, or just play around with it to suit your mood on the particular day that you make it.

SERVES 4 TO 6

3 tbsp extra-virgin olive oil

1 lb luganica, casing removed, crumbled

1 large red onion, cut into small dice

2 garlic cloves, thinly sliced

1 celery stalk, thinly sliced

½ fennel bulb, trimmed and cut into medium dice

Pinch saffron

1 cup dry white wine

2 tsp tomato paste

1 cup canned crushed tomatoes

2 tbsp all-purpose flour

2 cups Brodo (page 49), or any tasty low-sodium chicken broth

1. In a Dutch oven or deep skillet, heat the olive oil over medium-high heat. Add the sausage and sauté until lightly browned but still pink inside, about 8 minutes. Use a wooden spoon to break it up into small chunks. Remove from the pan using a slotted spoon and set aside.

2. Add the onion to the pan and cook over medium heat until translucent, 4 to 5 minutes. Stir in the garlic, celery, fennel, and saffron. Cook for 2 to 3 minutes and then return the sausage to the pan. Stir in the wine, tomato paste, and crushed tomatoes. Simmer over low heat for 5 minutes and mix in the flour. Add the broth and gently simmer over low heat until the vegetables and sausage are tender, about 30 minutes.

||||||||||||||||
RECIPE NOTE

No one really agrees about where luganica sausage originated. It is often said that the recipe was first made by the Lucani, an ancient Italian people. It remains a mystery to this day where exactly the sausage was first made, however, and each region in Italy will tell you that it is their recipe, whether they know it as luganica or luganega or longaniza.

Pasta Bazzoffia

Roman Spring Vegetable "Ragù" with Pasta

I ATE THIS dish many years ago just outside Rome, where it proved a very appropriate "welcome" to spring. It was served very simply—just peas, fava beans, and artichoke ragu, with a slightly soupy consistency, topped with a lightly scrambled egg. It was amazing. Garlic scapes are the shoots that grow up early in the spring from garlic that was planted the previous fall. They have a pungent aroma, unlike anything else. Try this dish even if you can't find them (just omit them from the dish), but if you can find a source, enjoy them in this dish during the short season they are available.

SERVES 4

3 tbsp extra-virgin olive oil, plus more as needed

4 green onions, minced

2 spring garlic scapes

½ cup coarsely chopped flat-leaf parsley

8 fresh young artichoke hearts, cleaned and cut into eighths

1 cup fresh shelled peas

1 cup fresh young fava beans

1 tbsp all-purpose flour

1 cup water

Salt and freshly ground black pepper, as needed

1 lb short tubular pasta such as tubettini, small penne, etc.

1 cup freshly grated Pecorino Romano D.O.P.

1. In an ample skillet, warm the olive oil over low heat. Add the onions, garlic scapes, and parsley and sauté until translucent, about 5 minutes. Add the artichoke wedges, peas, and fava beans and let cook until very hot, about 4 minutes. Sprinkle in the flour and stir to mix it with the vegetables. Add the water and let simmer over low heat until the artichokes are tender, about 20 minutes. (This ragù freezes well, and will keep in the freezer for up to 2 months or more, or you can cool the sauce and transfer to storage containers.)

2. Bring 5 quarts of water to boil in a large pot. Stir in salt to taste and the pasta, and cook over high heat until it is al dente. (Cooking times will vary according to shape; consult the directions on your package.) Drain and transfer it to the skillet, tossing to combine the pasta and sauce well. Let it to cook together over medium heat until creamy, about 4 minutes.

3. Take the skillet off the heat and add more olive oil to taste, the grated cheese, and salt and pepper to taste. Serve at once.

Rotolo di Pasta Ripieno

Stuffed Pasta Roll

YOU MAY USE any kind of stuffing for this dish; this is a meat one, but if you prefer, use ricotta mixed with any greens you have available. The eggs added to the stuffing hold the roulade together after you cut into it. This dish can be prepared the day before you plan to serve it, making it a good choice for a dinner party, leaving you free to enjoy your guests.

SERVES 6

2 oz dried porcini mushrooms

2 tsp butter, plus as needed to grease pan

4 oz pancetta, small dice

½ cup minced onion

½ lb chicken liver

½ lb lean veal, diced

½ lb sweet Italian sausage, casing removed, crumbled

½ cup coarsely chopped fresh flat-leaf parsley

1 tsp chopped fresh sage leaves

1 tsp chopped fresh rosemary leaves

1 cup dry white wine

½ lb fresh spinach leaves

Water or broth, as needed

Salt and freshly ground black pepper, as needed

4 large eggs

1 cup freshly grated Parmigiano-Reggiano cheese

1 recipe Fresh Pasta (page 99), rolled into an 8 × 12 sheet

2 cups Quick Tomato Sauce (page 102)

1. Rehydrate the porcini in water for 1 hour, drain, and then chop.

2. In a 4-quart Dutch oven or large deep skillet with a cover, melt the butter over medium-high heat. Add the pancetta and onion and sauté until lightly colored, 5 to 6 minutes. Add the chicken liver, veal, porcini, and the sausage. When the meat starts changing color, about 4 minutes, add the parsley, sage, and rosemary and sauté for 2 minutes. Add the wine, spinach, and the chopped mushrooms; cover, and allow it to cook for 30 to 45 minutes, stirring occasionally to prevent the mixture from sticking to the bottom of the pan. (If necessary, add a little water or broth to moisten.) Remove from heat, allow to cool, and then season with salt and pepper as needed.

3. In a bowl, combine the cooked meat mixture, eggs, and ½ cup of the grated cheese. Transfer to the bowl of a food processor and grind. Set aside.

4. Lightly dampen a piece of cheesecloth or a clean kitchen towel and spread it out on your work surface. Place the sheet of pasta on top of the cheesecloth. Spread the stuffing to a thickness of ¼ inch over the pasta, leaving a ½-inch border. Roll up the pasta and wrap it with the cheesecloth. Tie each of the ends securely with kitchen twine, then lightly tie in four parts, like preparing a roast. *(recipe continues on next page)*

5. Fill a pot with enough water to cover the *rotolo* (pasta roll). Hold onto each end and lower it into the pot. Cook over very low heat for about 1 hour.

6. Preheat the oven to 375°F. Select a baking dish large enough to accommodate the rotolo, and grease with butter.

7. Transfer the rotolo to the pan and allow it to cool slightly. Carefully remove the cheese-cloth or towel. Using a sharp, long knife, cut the rotolo into ½-inch-thick slices. Arrange the slices in the baking dish and pour the tomato sauce over it. Sprinkle the remaining grated cheese on top. Bake until the top is lightly browned, about 10 to 15 minutes. Serve hot with additional sauce on the side.

Trenette con Càpperi, Pendolini, Olive e Rucola

Trenette with Capers, Tomatoes, Olives, and Arugula

I LOVE PASTA dishes that are quick to make but still taste and look fantastic. Add more or less of the hot chile, try different types of tomatoes or bitter greens. Add roasted peppers, anchovies, any kind of nuts, or sun-dried tomatoes. Most of the dish can be put together from pantry staples you may already have on hand for an easy dinner with friends—even on short notice.

SERVES 4

1 lb cherry tomatoes, halved, seeded and chopped

½ cup extra-virgin olive oil, plus as needed

2 garlic cloves, peeled and crushed

1 small fresh or dried hot red chile

⅔ cup mixed black and green olives, pitted and coarsely chopped

2 tbsp brine-packed capers, rinsed and drained

½ cup packed arugula, coarsely chopped

Salt and freshly ground black pepper, as needed

1 lb trenette pasta or linguine

1. In a serving bowl, combine the tomatoes, olive oil, garlic, chile pepper, olives, capers, and arugula. Mix well and allow it to rest at room temperature for 20 minutes to develop flavor.

2. Bring 5 quarts water to a rolling boil. Stir in salt as needed and the pasta. Cook over high heat until the pasta is "al dente," about 8 to 10 minutes (check the directions on your package for cooking times). Drain, reserving a few table-spoons of the cooking water. Toss with the arugula mixture. Season to taste with salt, pepper, and a drizzle of olive oil. (If necessary, add some of the reserved pasta water to keep it moist.) Serve at once.

Pennette Rigate con Pomodoro Crudo e Sylvetta

Small Penne Pasta with Fresh Tomato and Wild Arugula

SYLVETTA IS A wild arugula, a relative of the cultivated green, but with a wildfire pungency. It is more heat tolerant and much more cold tolerant than standard arugula, making it a critical component of winter green salad mixes.

SERVES 4

¾ lb ripe but firm grape, cherry, or pear tomatoes

3 tbsp extra-virgin olive oil

Salt and freshly ground black pepper, as needed

½ cup packed fresh basil leaves, torn into small pieces

Pinch of fresh or dry oregano, as needed

2 oz ricotta salata (aged ricotta)

1 lb pennette rigate

1 cup packed sylvetta or baby arugula leaves

1. Wash and slice the tomatoes into a large salad bowl. If there is too much juice from the sliced tomatoes, drain the excess. (Too much juice can make your pasta too watery.)

2. Dress the tomatoes with the oil, a very little salt (the *ricotta salata* tends to be quite salty by nature), pepper, basil, and oregano. Grate half of the ricotta (using a cheese grater or micro plane with large holes) on top of the tomatoes and set aside for 3 to 5 minutes.

3. Meanwhile cook the pasta "al dente" following the directions on the package, drain, and add to the tomatoes, combining well. Complete the dish by grating the rest of the ricotta salata over the pasta and folding in the arugula. Serve immediately while the pasta is still quite hot.

IIIIIIIIIIIIIIIII
RECIPE NOTES

This is one of my favorite summer dishes. It only takes a few minutes to make, and the taste is just phenomenal. You may add other ingredients as you like, such as grilled eggplant or zucchini (or any summer vegetables you wish), or fresh mozzarella cut into small dice.

For the oregano, if you can find fresh, great; if not, try to find a good-quality variety that comes dried on the stem, still intact; the flavor will change the way you think about dried oregano. The oregano that comes from Sicily, for example, has a great strong flavor, and you need to use much less than usual.

Gnocchi di Ricotta e Ortiche al Cucchiaio

"Spoon" Ricotta and Nettle Dumplings

EVERY REGION IN Italy has its own version of this recipe; the name might change, though, or the name from one place might mean something completely different in another. I still get confused at times, so I can only imagine how it is for people who were not born in Italy. For instance, some people call this style of gnocchi *gnudi* (naked) because the mixture is very similar to the stuffing you could use to fill ravioli or other stuffed pastas. Some people will refer to these gnocchi as *strangolapreti* (priest chokers). Sometimes they are made with stale bread that was soaked in milk, then blended with flour and eggs, and on it goes! You may replace the nettles called for here with any other soft greens (spinach, parsley, basil, dandelion, any fresh herbs, etc.). You may also add some citrus zest and other spices if you wish. Make sure you use the best ricotta you can find. Once you get the feeling for this type of gnocchi, it is a very quick dish to make, and very tasty.

SERVES 4

2 cups (heaping) nettles or
    spinach, young leaves only,
    stems removed

2 cups fresh ricotta, drained

1 cup crumbled fresh goat cheese or
    mascarpone

2 large eggs

1 egg yolk

Pinch of nutmeg

1½ cups freshly grated Parmigiano-
    Reggiano, divided

3 tbsp extra-virgin olive oil, divided

Salt and freshly ground black pep-
    per, as needed

¾ cup all-purpose flour, plus as
    needed

FOR THE SAUCE

1 cup (2 sticks) unsalted butter

6 fresh large sage leaves

1. In a kettle, boil enough water to cover the nettles or spinach. Blanch the leaves for few seconds. Drain, shock in cold water, and drain again. Purée in a food processor or chop very finely by hand.

2. Use a fine mesh sieve to drain the excess moisture from the ricotta. Place the ricotta into a bowl and mix in the goat cheese or mascarpone, eggs, egg yolk, nettles or spinach, nutmeg, ¾ cup of grated cheese, 2 tablespoons of olive oil, salt, and pepper. Blend well with a wooden spoon. Slowly add the flour and mix until combined, but take care not to overwork it. (The quantity of flour given in this recipe is only an approximation; more may be needed if the ricotta is very wet.) If you are not using the dumplings immediately, refrigerate them until ready to use.

3. Melt the butter together with the sage and keep warm.

4. In a large pot, bring 4 quarts of water to a rolling boil. As soon as you are ready to cook the dumplings, add the remaining 1 tablespoon of olive oil and 2 tablespoons of salt to the water. Using a small ice cream scoop, scoop up the mixture and make dumplings about the size of a walnut. (Alternatively, let the mixture chill for 1 hour, and then form the dumplings with your hands, making sure to keep them well-floured at all times to prevent them from getting sticky.)

5. To cook the dumplings, slip them into the boiling water a few at a time. They are done when they float to the surface for one minute. Using a slotted spoon, gently remove the dumplings to a large serving platter and pour the butter sauce over them. Sprinkle with the remaining grated cheese and serve at once.

SPAGHETTI AL VINO ROSSO

SPAGHETTI WITH RED WINE AND PECORINO

THIS UNUSUAL PASTA dish from Umbria is cooked more like a risotto than a typical pasta dish. As the pasta cooks, the wine infuses it with flavor and the color deepens to a rich chestnut color.

SERVES 4

1 lb spaghetti

Salt, as needed

¼ cup extra-virgin olive oil, plus more
  for drizzling before serving

3 cups good quality light, dry red wine

¾ cup aged D.O.P. Pecorino Toscano
  or Parmigiano-Reggiano

1. Bring 5 quarts of water to a rapid boil. Stir in the pasta and a generous pinch of salt. Cook for 6 to 8 minutes, depending on the thickness of the spaghetti. Drain, reserving some of the cooking water.

2. In the meantime, in an ample skillet, warm the oil over medium heat. Add the pasta and toss. Gradually add the wine, ½ cup at a time, tossing continually, until the wine is absorbed by the pasta. When the wine is almost entirely absorbed, add the cheese, and combine well. Serve very hot.

Bigoli e Sarde

Venetian-style Pasta with Sardines

MY PARENTS WOULD make this dish for us every month—it was a ritual when I was growing up. My mother and father worked as a team, and it would take them the whole day to prepare. My father was in charge of making the *bigoli*, and he would hang the cut pasta on the back of the chairs to dry for a few hours before cooking. We still aren't sure exactly what he added to make his bigoli so good—a little bit of wine in the dough, perhaps, or not too much whole wheat flour—whatever his secrets, we could never pry them out of him. My mother tells me little secrets here and there, but I don't think even she remembers for sure. I just know that his bigoli were the best, and nobody will ever be able to change my mind about that!

SERVES 4

14 oz sardines, packed in salt, bones removed, rinsed well

¾ cup dry white wine

¾ cup extra-virgin olive oil

2 large red onions, minced

¼ fennel bulb, roughly chopped

⅓ cup golden raisins, softened in warm water, drained, and chopped

½ cup chopped fresh flat-leaf parsley

Freshly ground black pepper, as needed

1 lb whole wheat spaghetti, linguini, or other long, thick shape

1. Wash the sardines very well, making sure you remove the bones, head if any, and impurities. Separate the fillets and discard the rest. Soak the fillets in half of the wine and set aside.

2. In a sauté pan heat the olive oil with the onions over medium-high heat and cook until the onions start turning a light brown, about 8 minutes. Remove the sardines from the white wine (discard the wine they have been soaking in), and cut them into medium pieces. Add the sardines to the onion along with the fennel, the raisins, and half of the parsley; stir to combine. Season with black pepper only, as the sardines are quite salty. Let cook for 2 minutes and then add the remaining wine. Continue cooking until the wine slightly evaporates, but not completely, about 5 minutes. Pour in enough water to just cover the onion-sardine mixture and let cook very slowly over very low heat, until the onion and fennel are almost dissolved, resulting in a chunky sauce, about 30 minutes.

3. Cook the pasta al dente, drain it, and pour into the bowl where the "salsa" is. Toss well, add the remaining parsley, and serve immediately.

Spaghetti al Pesto delle Lipari

Spaghetti with Pesto from the Lipari Islands

THIS RECIPE COMES from Lipari, part of an archipelago of volcanic islands to the north of Sicily. At certain times of the year, fresh tomatoes may be a bit watery; let them rest briefly in a colander after you remove the seeds, to allow any excess moisture to drain away before adding them to the pesto.

SERVES 4

6 vine-ripened San Marzano tomatoes

3 tbsp peeled and crushed almonds

2 tbsp pine nuts

2 tbsp chopped walnuts

1 serrano chile or 1 dry hot red chile, crushed

1 garlic clove, peeled and crushed

10 fresh mint leaves

3 tbsp extra-virgin olive oil

Salt and freshly ground black pepper, as needed

½ cup freshly grated Pecorino Romano D.O.P

1 lb spaghetti, fusilli, or farfalle

1. Blanch the tomatoes in enough boiling water to cover until their skins loosen, about 30 seconds. Cool them in cold water. Use a paring knife to lift off their skin. Cut the tomatoes in half and push out the excess seeds with your finger or a small spoon.

2. In the bowl of a food processor, combine the almonds, pine nuts, walnuts, hot pepper to taste, and garlic. Process for 1 minute or until all the ingredients are very fine and homogeneous. Stop the machine, add the tomatoes, mint, oil, and salt to taste. Process for 20 seconds to evenly combine the pesto. Transfer to a bowl large enough to accommodate the cooked pasta.

3. Fold in the grated cheese and combine well. Season with salt and pepper, as needed.

4. Bring 5 quarts of water to a rolling boil and stir in salt as needed and the pasta. Cook over high heat until the pasta is "al dente," about 10 minutes, stirring occasionally. Drain, reserving some of the cooking water.

5. Toss the pasta with the pesto. (Moisten with a few tablespoons of the cooking water, if necessary.) Mix well and serve immediately.

Fusilli al Pesto di Rucola e Nocciole

"Corkscrew" Pasta with Arugula and Hazelnut Pesto

SOMETIMES, WRITING RECIPES is challenging for me. For instance, how much parsley should I write down? I use my eyes, hands, and nose to guide me, and then taste and adjust as the dish develops. Use the amounts given here as a starting point, but remember to let your own palate be your guide—some ingredients have stronger flavors at certain times of the year.

SERVES 4 TO 6

3 packed cups arugula leaves, washed and dried

⅓ cup chopped toasted hazelnuts

⅓ cup chopped fresh flat-leaf parsley

1 garlic clove, peeled and crushed

⅓ cup fresh sheep or goat milk ricotta

¼ cup extra-virgin olive oil, plus as needed

Salt and freshly ground black pepper, as needed

1 lb fusilli pasta

1 pt red and yellow grape tomatoes, halved

½ cup freshly grated Parmigiano-Reggiano cheese

1. Bring enough water to boil to blanch the arugula. Blanch the leaves quickly in the hot water. Drain and immediately shock in ice cold water to prevent discoloration. Drain again. Squeeze the arugula well to remove any excess water, then chop coarsely.

2. In the bowl of a food processor, combine the arugula, nuts (setting aside 1 tablespoon for garnish), parsley, garlic, ricotta, olive oil, and salt and pepper to taste, and puree for a few seconds. Gradually add some additional olive oil, just enough to form a creamy, but not oily, consistency. Transfer to a serving bowl, stir in additional salt and pepper to taste, and set aside.

3. Bring 5 quarts water to a rolling boil. Add the pasta and cook until it is al dente, about 12 minutes, stirring occasionally. Drain the pasta and reserve the cooking liquid.

4. Toss the pasta with the pesto. Add as much of the reserved pasta cooking water as necessary to moisten, and toss. Toss in the tomatoes and grated cheese. Distribute the pasta onto individual serving plates and garnish with the reserved hazelnuts.

||||||||||||||||
RECIPE NOTES

The pesto in this dish is an alternative to the regular basil pesto; it uses arugula instead of basil for a more pungent flavor than what we are used to, and replaces the pine nuts with hazelnuts for a slightly different taste. In the spirit of expanding your pesto repertoire, here are my suggestions for a spinach pesto: Replace the arugula with an equal amount of spinach (spinach is usually easier to find throughout the year), and add some cooked onion and prosciutto to the spinach to bolster the flavor of the pesto.

PACCHERI CON PESCE E CARCIOFI

LARGE RIGATONI WITH FISH AND ARTICHOKES

YOU MAY USE any kind of firm white-fleshed fish in this recipe, as well as crab meat, lobster, or shrimp. You can also try substituting zucchini, peas, chopped fresh tomatoes, or beans for the artichokes.

SERVES 6

Juice of ½ lemon

8 baby artichokes

½ cup extra-virgin olive oil

3 garlic cloves, peeled and thinly sliced

½ tsp chopped fresh hot red pepper, as needed

12 to 14 oz skinless firm white-fleshed fish filets, cut into 2-inch chunks

½ cup chopped fresh flat-leaf parsley leaves

½ cup dry white wine

Salt and freshly ground black pepper, as needed

1 lb paccheri pasta (rigatoni)

½ cup fresh basil leaves, torn into small pieces

1. Fill a bowl large enough to hold the artichokes half full with cold water. Add the lemon juice. Clean the baby artichokes (see page 154). Cut them into eights, cover, and set them aside in the lemon water.

2. In an ample skillet large enough to accommodate the pasta, warm the olive oil, garlic, and hot pepper over low heat. Sauté until aromatic, about 1 minute. Add the artichokes and cook until nearly tender, 10 to 12 minutes. Toss in the fish and ¼ cup of the parsley. Pour in the wine, season with salt and pepper, and cook over low heat to allow the alcohol to evaporate, about 5 minutes more.

3. In the meantime, bring 5 quarts of water to a rolling boil. Add the pasta and 2 tablespoons of salt. Cook over high heat, stirring occasionally to prevent sticking, until the pasta is "al dente," 8 to 10 minutes, depending on the thickness of your rigatoni. Drain, reserving about ½ cup of the pasta water.

4. Add the pasta to the skillet with the fish and artichoke sauce. Toss together well and cook over medium heat to combine the flavors, 2 to 3 minutes. If pasta seems dry, add some of the reserved pasta cooking water to moisten. Just before serving, add the remaining parsley, the fresh basil, and drizzle with some extra-virgin olive oil. Season to taste with salt and pepper and serve immediately.

Pasta con Cozze e Fagioli

Pasta with Mussels and Beans

YOU COULD USE fresh pasta in this dish, such as *tagliatelle* or *pappardelle*, cut into bite-sized pieces, or a dried pasta that you've cooked halfway, such as *tubettini* or *pennette*. As the pasta cooks with the mussels, it will absorb their flavor.

SERVES 4

2 oz dry cannellini beans (or 2 cups cooked or canned cannellini beans, drained and rinsed)

1 fresh bay leaf

2 fresh rosemary sprigs

5 garlic cloves

4 dozen mussels

¾ cup extra-virgin olive oil

1 cup dry white wine

2 chopped fresh tarragon leaves

1 lb fresh or pre-cooked dried egg pasta

Salt and freshly ground black pepper, as needed

¼ cup chopped fresh flat-leaf parsley

4 toasted bread slices

1. (If you are using prepared beans, skip this step.) Prepare the beans a day in advance: Wash them and cover with cold water. Soak overnight. To cook the beans, place them in a pot with enough cold water to cover them by 3 inches. Add the bay leaf, rosemary, and 2 cloves of garlic that have been smashed. Bring to a boil. Reduce to a simmer and cook the beans over low heat for about 1 hour. Skim the foam that might come to surface during cooking. Remove the bay leaf and discard.

2. In the meantime, scrub the mussels and pull out their beards. Discard any open ones. Rinse them well and set aside.

3. Thinly slice the remaining garlic. In a deep pot large enough to hold the mussels when they are open, warm half of the olive oil over medium heat with the sliced garlic until softened, about 2 minutes. Add the mussels to the pan along with the wine, cover tightly, and cook until the mussels open, about 8 to 10 minutes.

4. Drain the mussels and reserve the liquid. Remove the mussels from their shells, leaving a few intact for garnish.

5. In a food processor, puree half of the beans along with the cooked rosemary and garlic, the liquid of the mussels, the tarragon, and some of the liquid from the beans. (This should result in a semi-soupy sauce.) In a large sauce pot, bring this liquid to a boil. Stir in the pasta and cook over medium heat until the sauce is thickened and creamy, about 5 minutes. (If necessary, add more liquid during cooking.) Just before the pasta is cooked, stir in the mussels and the remaining whole beans. Cook for an additional 2 to 3 minutes. Season with salt and pepper to taste.

6. Ladle the soup into individual serving bowls. Garnish each bowl with the reserved mussels. Drizzle with olive oil to taste, sprinkle with parsley, and serve very hot, accompanied by the toasted bread.

"*Il pesce e il riso vivono nell'aqua
e muoiono nel vino.*"

Fish and rice are born in water
and die in wine.

— ITALIAN PROVERB

ITALIAN GASTRONOMY IN THE UNITED STATES

THERE WAS A TIME not so long ago in the United States when the mention of Italian food conjured up some very specific images: a red-checkered tablecloth featuring as its centerpiece an empty *fiasco* of Chianti with a candle dripping wax all over; a big bowl of spaghetti with red sauce and meatballs, covered with a mountain of grated cheese; or a nice dish of chicken *parmigiana* with a side of angel hair pasta; maybe a nice glass of red wine; and a basket of garlic bread.

I remember my first experience in an Italian-American restaurant when I first moved to the United States 16 years ago. There were pictures on the wall of the Leaning Tower of Pisa, the Coliseum in Rome, the Bay of Naples, and the Greek temples in Sicily. To me it looked like a travel agency, since most of the pictures had an inscription on the bottom that read "Alitalia Airlines." The rest of the walls were festooned with colorful lights, fake salami and cured meats, pictures of Luciano Pavarotti and Sofia Loren, and Italian flags in all different shapes and sizes. The table was set with the stereotypical red-checkered cloth. The centerpiece was a bottle of San Pellegrino water. The server greeted us very warmly and brought a basket of bread covered with sesame seeds right away. Then he brought a large menu with a several laminated sheets.

I got lost trying to take in words that, even though they sounded Italian, I had never heard before: *fra diavolo, scampi, marinara, piccata, francese, alfredo, a lá vodka,* and so on. All the while my friend was making sounds of pleasure as he read the menu. Was this for real? Was he looking at the same menu I was?

When the server approached us to take our order, my friend already knew what he wanted, but I, on the other hand, had no idea. He ordered for me: Chicken Francese with spaghetti on the side.

After a short while an oval plate came to the table with two pieces of chicken drowning in a brown buttery sauce and spaghetti with a scoop of bright red sauce on top. All I tasted was the overpowering sauce and not the *materia prima* (prime material)—that is to say, the chicken. With everything all mixed together this way, my palette couldn't make sense of the dish. The pasta was even more shocking: it had neither body nor texture, and just melted away in my mouth. I couldn't finish my meal, which left me both hungry and depressed. My friend asked what was wrong and I told him I didn't

like it. He seemed a little offended, so I simply answered that if he wanted to try real Italian food he should come over to my Mom's house. He did, and it completely changed his experience of Italian food. He hasn't set foot in that restaurant since.

How did those stereotypes, found to this day in some Italian-American restaurants, get their start? As an Italian and food lover, I had to investigate.

When Italian immigrants settled in the United States they tried to shed the traditions they had observed in their villages and towns. It was very important for them to learn the lifestyle, the language, and the attitude of the New World. They were trying to fit in. They invested all that they had in chasing the American Dream.

As they integrated into their new country and the ties to their homeland became more tenuous, Italians in America started blending culinary principles from all over Italy, mixing in some uniquely American concepts along the way, to create the dishes that define Italian-American food.

In this country, restaurant-goers traditionally looked for quantity and large portions. In response, the *primo piatto* (the first plate, or pasta course) was served alongside the *secondo piatto* (the second plate, or the main course). Italian-American food might be lucrative for some restaurants, but it certainly is not authentic Italian food.

What is authentic Italian food? I would define it as a widely respected, simple, sometimes elegant, yet often rustic cuisine that depends for its success upon fresh, quality ingredients prepared in such a way that the flavor is enhanced, but never masked. Freshness is an important factor for both quality and for health. The typical Italian person shops on a daily basis. The ritual of shopping in stores that each have their own specialty is still alive and practiced throughout Italy. Some items must be purchased not only on daily basis and from a specific shop, but also at a specific time of the day. The marketplace fills with goods such as bread, fish, fruits, vegetables, and eggs. Shoppers stroll through the market where they smell, touch, taste, and, of course, haggle over the price.

Quality over quantity and small portions are authentic Italian. We constantly use terms such as *pizzicare* or *stuzzicare*—words that mean to nibble—when we talk about food. Italians enjoy three or four courses at both lunch and dinner: a *primo piatto* (a pasta or soup), *secondo piatto* (a main dish served with a *contorno*, or side dish), and perhaps some cheese and fruit to follow. It sounds like a lot, but in reality it's all about small servings of foods of the best possible quality. Italians may live to eat, but in reality we are not heavy eaters. My grandmother always told me to "leave the table a little hungry." That is authentic Italian, too.

CHAPTER FOUR

SECONDI E CONTORNI

Main Dishes and Accompaniments

UOVA IN PURGATORIO

EGGS IN PURGATORY

This simple egg dish is an amazing, flavorful dish as long as you use the very freshest eggs and the best good quality tomatoes. This is no place to use generic canned tomatoes!

SERVES 4

2 lb ripe plum tomatoes

2 tbsp extra-virgin olive oil

2 garlic cloves, peeled and thinly sliced

1 tbsp chopped parsley

8 basil leaves, fresh, torn in pieces

Kosher salt and freshly ground black pepper, as needed

8 large eggs

8 slices grilled or toasted bread

1. Blanch the tomatoes in boiling water for 30 seconds, shock them in cold water, then peel the skin. Cut the tomatoes in half, remove most of the seeds, and then cut them in large dice; set aside.

2. Heat the oil in a sauté pan or saucepan that has a cover over medium heat with the garlic. Just before the garlic starts to take on any color, about 1 minute, add the tomatoes, parsley, and basil. Season with salt and pepper, bring to a simmer over low heat, and let cook for 10 min-utes, until tomatoes become "saucy," but are still a little chunky.

3. Break the eggs, one at the time, into a cup or dish and then gently slide them, one at the time and without breaking the yolks, on top of tomato sauce. Try to keep them separated.

4. Cover the pan and let cook gently for 3 to 4 minutes, until the eggs are done, but still soft. Immediately serve them on a large round plate with the tomato sauce. Serve the grilled or toasted bread on the side.

|||||||||||||||||

RECIPE NOTE

Instead of cooking the eggs whole, you may also scramble the eggs into the tomato sauce and serve as they are.

|||||||||||||||||||||||||||

WINE SUGGESTION

Albana Secco

Coda di Rospo ai Pomodorini Pendolini Misti

Monkfish with Fresh Tomatoes

YOU MAY USE any other fresh fish available at your market. If the fish you choose has a flakier texture than the monkfish called for here, it is best to make the sauce first, and then add the fish just at the last moment. If the monkfish fillet is very big, slice it into medallions for better cooking. Avoid very small fillets because they will cook too fast. You can serve this dish with a good polenta, pilaf rice, or even some boiled new potatoes.

SERVES 6

2 lb monkfish filet

Salt and freshly ground black pepper, as needed

3 tbsp extra-virgin olive oil

3 garlic cloves, peeled and crushed

1 red onion, thinly sliced

1 cup dry white wine

2 pt grape or cherry tomatoes, halved

½ cup fresh basil leaves, torn into small pieces

1 tbsp salt-cured capers

¼ cup pitted olives, different varieties

¼ cup fresh coarsely chopped flat-leaf parsley

1. Season the monkfish to taste with salt and pepper.

2. Warm the oil in a large skillet over medium-high heat. Add the fish to the pan and sauté on both sides until lightly browned, about 2 minutes per side, depending on the thickness of the filets. Remove the fish and transfer it to a plate. Set aside. Add the garlic and onion to the pan and sauté them until they are translucent, about 5 to 6 minutes.

3. Return the fish to the pan, add the wine, and let the alcohol evaporate partially, about 3 minutes. Stir in the tomatoes, basil, capers, olives, and parsley. Cover and cook over medium heat until the fish is done, about 8 to 10 minutes. Remove the pan from the heat and serve at once.

|||||||||||||||
RECIPE NOTES

If the sauce is too loose due to the water content of the tomatoes, remove the fish, let the sauce reduce to the right consistency, and then serve. Once the capers and olives simmer with the tomatoes, they tend to release salt. Make sure you season the sauce only at the very end, and only if necessary.

|||||||||||||||||||||
WINE SUGGESTION

White: Vermentino | Red: Carignano

Pesce in Brodetto Rapido con Scarola e Patate Gialle

Market Fish with Escarole and Yellow Potatoes

CHOOSING THE RIGHT fish for this dish is important; try a firmer-fleshed fish such as haddock or cod, or ask your fishmonger for advice on what from the day's catch might work well. In Italy, any fish that lives "close to the cliffs" is thought to be excellent for soup, but those fish often have a lot of bones. The most traditional (and flavorful) way to make this dish would be cooking the fish still on the bone, so long as you and your guests don't mind the extra effort—the difference in flavor is worth the trouble.

SERVES 6

2 lb white, firm-fleshed fish filets

Salt and freshly ground black pepper, as needed

Pinch of saffron threads, lightly crushed

1 tbsp Sambuca

2 tbsp tomato paste

3 tbsp extra-virgin olive oil

2 tsp minced shallot

4 garlic cloves, peeled and sliced

¼ cup thinly sliced fresh fennel

1 carrot, thinly sliced

2 celery stalks, peeled and thinly sliced

2 lb Yukon Gold potatoes, peeled and thinly sliced

¾ lb escarole, washed and coarsely chopped

2 fresh thyme sprigs

1 fresh bay leaf

¼ cup fresh basil leaves, torn into small pieces

½ cup coarsely chopped fresh flat-leaf parsley

¾ cup dry white wine

12 oz crushed tomatoes

6 sea scallops

2 lb small clams, well cleaned and purged of grit

1 lb mussels, debearded, well cleaned and purged of grit

1 lb shrimp or lobster, cleaned and deveined

6 slices bread

1 clove garlic, peeled and halved

Extra-virgin olive oil, as needed

1. Season the fish filets with salt and pepper to taste and place them in a large bowl with the saffron, Sambuca, and tomato paste. Cover with plastic wrap and refrigerate until ready to use.

2. *To prepare the brodetto:* In a 5-quart saucepan, warm the olive oil over medium-low heat. Add the shallot and sauté until tender, about 1 minute. Stir in the garlic, fennel, carrot, and celery. Let cook for 5 minutes. Add the potatoes, escarole, herbs, and wine and continue to cook for 5 minutes. Stir in the tomatoes and their juices, and bring to a very slow simmer. Cook over the lowest possible heat until hot, about 5 minutes. Add the fish filets along with all the juices left in the bowl. Cook for 5 minutes. Drop in the scallops, followed by the clams, mussels, and then the shrimp or lobster, all the while cooking over very low heat. (Add water as necessary to prevent the contents of the pot from drying out.) When the clams and mussels have opened and all the seafood is cooked, remove the soup from the heat. Discard any shells that did not open. Check the seasoning and add salt and pepper if needed.

3. While the brodetto is cooking, toast the bread slices. Rub each slice on both sides with a peeled, halved garlic clove, and drizzle with olive oil to taste. Check the seasoning of the brodetto and adjust if needed. Divide the bread among six plates and ladle the brodetto over each slice. Drizzle with more of the olive oil just before serving.

||||||||||||||||||||||||

WINE SUGGESTION

White: Nuragus | Red: Valpolicella

Spadellata di Cozze con Fagioli

Mussels Cooked in Their Own Broth with Beans

BUY THE MUSSELS from a good source to make sure they are extremely fresh—opt for Prince Edward Island ("P. E. I.") mussels if you can find them. Wash the mussels well and debeard them. You could also use good-quality canned mussels, but it's much better to use fresh.

SERVES 6

¼ cup extra-virgin olive oil. plus additional as needed

¼ cup minced shallot

5 garlic cloves, thinly sliced

½ cup coarsely chopped flat-leaf parsley

Hot pepper, dry or fresh, as needed

5 lb mussels, cleaned, washed, and debearded

1 tsp freshly ground black pepper

½ cup white wine

2½ cups Quick Tomato Sauce, (page 102) or crushed tomatoes, juices drained

¼ cup chopped basil

1½ cup cooked white cannellini beans (page 149)

Salt, as needed

6 large slices bread, grilled or toasted, and rubbed with garlic

1. In a large pan with a cover, heat the oil with the shallot over low heat. Once the shallot is translucent, about 1 minute, add the garlic, parsley, and hot pepper to taste. Let cook for 2 minutes to develop flavor.

2. Add the mussels and black pepper; toss to combine. Add the wine, let simmer for 1 minute, and then add the tomato sauce or crushed tomatoes, basil, and the cooked beans.

3. Cover and cook until the mussels have fully opened, about 8 minutes. Discard any unopened shells, and adjust the seasoning with salt and pepper, if necessary.

4. Divide the mussels among 6 serving plates or serve in a big bowl placed in the center of the table to serve them family-style. Pour all the sauce from the cooking on top of mussels, and drizzle with some olive oil. Serve very hot with grilled or toasted bread rubbed with garlic.

IIIIIIIIIIIIIIII
RECIPE NOTES

You can substitute Great Northern, navy, or even cranberry beans for the cannellini beans, depending on your taste.

The best way to rub your bread with garlic is to take a whole garlic clove, slice it in half, and, holding the tip of the garlic, rub it on the toasted bread once, just enough to leave the scent of the garlic on the bread, more if you like really strong garlic flavor.

IIIIIIIIIIIIIIIIIIIIII
WINE SUGGESTION

White: Montonico | Red: Gaglioppo

Polipo Affogato con Patate Gialle

Drowned Octopus with Yellow Potatoes

IF YOUR OCTOPUS is very fresh, it will be naturally salty, so make sure you adjust the seasoning accordingly. There is a belief among fishermen along the Riviera in Italy that when you catch an octopus, you should kill it against the cliffs, then rub its tentacles hard on the rocks to give it a tender texture when it cooks. Some cooks believe that you should put a couple of corks in the cooking water to tenderize the octopus. Yet another belief is that, before you drop the octopus into hot water, you should let it "feel" the water with its tentacles first, until they start to curl up, then release it into the water. I can't say if any of this could be scientifically proven, but tradition is very hard to change.

SERVES 4

4 lb octopus, defrosted if frozen

3 garlic cloves, crushed

1 fresh or dried hot red chile (see note)

22 oz peeled San Marzano tomatoes and their juices

1½ cups dry wine, red or white

½ cup extra-virgin olive oil

¾ cup chopped flat-leaf parsley

Salt, as needed

2½ lb Yukon Gold potatoes, cut into large cubes

1. Wash the octopus and place it in a tall, narrow casserole (preferably made of terracotta, but if not, use whatever tall narrow pot you have available) with the garlic, hot pepper, tomatoes, wine, olive oil, parsley, and a pinch of salt to taste.

2. Cover the casserole tightly, and let the octopus cook very, very slowly over low heat, for about 2 hours total. Half an hour before you are ready to remove the octopus from the heat, add the potatoes, making sure there is enough liquid in the casserole to cover them. Add some water if necessary. Serve the octopus with the potatoes in the same casserole you cook it in.

|||||||||||||||||
RECIPE NOTES

Many dishes in Italian cooking require a hot chile, whether green or red. If you can find fresh small red chiles, just make a small slit in the side of the chile before you place it in the pot; you can leave the chile in for your more adventurous guests to try. If you can't find fresh red chiles, try small dried chiles such as a Thai bird. And failing that, replace the chile called for here with ¼ teaspoon of red pepper flakes, the kind that you can sprinkle on your pizza at any self-respecting pizzeria. This recipe is good served cold or at room temperature. It also works as an appetizer.

|||||||||||||||||||||||
WINE SUGGESTION

White: Greco di Tufo | Red: Magliocco

Porchetta di Maiale "Povera"

"Poor Man's" Pork Roast

TRADITIONAL "POOR FOOD" like pig's feet and pork belly has enjoyed a newfound popularity in gastronomic circles. This is similar to a dish I had once outside of Rome, where *porchetta* is typically made with suckling pig. This dish goes wonderfully with a fresh *porcini* salad: Slice the mushrooms very thin, combine with some sliced radishes, dress with lemon, olive oil, and a little bit of parsley, and top with Parmesan shavings. Another noble mushroom you might consider for this delicious salad is *ovoli*, a very rare mushroom (they can be quite expensive), white in color with a hint of orange on the cap.

SERVES 6

3 pig's feet

¼ cup olive oil

1 medium onion, chopped

1 medium carrot, minced

1 celery stalk, minced

2 fresh bay leaves

2 marjoram sprigs, coarsely chopped

1 lb Yukon Gold potatoes, peeled
    and cut into medium dice

4 cups Brodo (page 49) or low-
    sodium meat or chicken broth

½ cup wild fennel sprigs (or fennel
    fronds)

Kosher salt and freshly ground
    black pepper, as needed

2 lb pork belly, cleaned

2 tbsp rosemary and 2 tbsp sage,
    chopped together

1. Preheat the oven to 325°F.

2. Starting with cold water to cover the pig's feet by 2 inches, bring them to a gentle simmer over low heat. Once the pig's feet are tender, about 1½ hours, remove and cut into pieces.

3. Heat the olive oil in a large pot or Dutch oven over medium heat. Add the onion, carrot, and celery, and cook until almost caramelized, about 8 minutes. Add the pig's feet, bay leaves, and marjoram, and let cook for 2 to 3 minutes. Add the potatoes and the broth and cook until the pig's feet are almost breaking apart, about 25 minutes. Allow to cool, then remove the bones from the pig's feet, add the wild fennel, and season with salt and pepper. This is the stuffing.

4. Open the pork belly flat and remove any large pieces of fat. Sprinkle with the rosemary and sage. Spread the stuffing on the belly. Roll it up lengthwise, tie tightly with twine, and roast at 325°F for about 1 hour or until the inside temperature reaches 165°F. Remove the pork from the oven and let it rest for 10 minutes or so.

5. Slice the pork belly, and serve with the fresh porcini salad mentioned above, or perhaps the Zucchine alle Erbette on page 147.

|||||||||||||||||||||
WINE SUGGESTION

White: Grillo | Red: Raboso

Coniglio all'Ischitana

Rabbit in Red Wine in the Style of Ischia

ISCHIA ISLAND IS currently a hot culinary destination, but for much of its history, the island was very poor. Some of the most well-known dishes on the island feature foods that were easy to forage or capture, like this traditional rabbit dish. Selective breeding of rabbits has been employed for many years on Ischia, in order to ensure a supply of high-quality meat.

SERVES 6

1 rabbit (about 3¼ lb), cut up, liver reserved

1 medium onion, chopped

2 carrots, cut into medium dice

2 celery stalks, cut into medium dice

2 garlic cloves, peeled and smashed

1 fresh bay leaf, torn into pieces

¼ cinnamon stick

2 cloves

1 bottle full-bodied dry red wine, such as Nebbiolo or Amarone

1 cup all-purpose flour

3 tbsp olive oil

1 tbsp unsalted butter

Salt and freshly ground black pepper, as needed

1. Wash the rabbit pieces under cold water and pat dry with paper toweling.

2. In a bowl, add the onion, carrots, celery, garlic, bay leaf, cinnamon, and cloves. Pour in the red wine and mix well. Add the rabbit pieces and cover with plastic wrap. Let marinate in the refrigerator for at least 12 hours.

3. When you are ready to cook, remove the rabbit from the marinade and pat dry with paper toweling. Strain the marinade, reserving the wine. Remove the bay leaves, cinnamon, and cloves and reserve. Roughly chop the vegetables and set aside.

4. Dredge the rabbit pieces in flour and shake off any excess. Heat a casserole, large enough to hold the meat, over low heat. Add the oil and butter. When the butter is melted, add the rabbit pieces and sauté until well colored on all sides. Remove the rabbit pieces using a slotted spoon and set aside. In the same casserole, add the vegetables from the marinade and cook until translucent, about 10 to 15 minutes.

5. Add back the rabbit pieces, season with salt and pepper, and pour in the wine reserved from the marinade. Add the reserved bay leaves, cinnamon, and cloves. Cover and gently bring to a simmer over low heat for about 1 hour; the meat should cook very slowly.

6. Chop the liver very fine and add it to the casserole. Let simmer for another 10 minutes. At the end of the cooking time, the wine should be completely absorbed and the sauce should be quite dense. To make the sauce more uniform, you may pass it through a food mill with the smallest disc. Serve the rabbit very hot, accompanied by Naughty Polenta (page 86), and perhaps a bottle of the same wine you used to cook the rabbit.

AGNELLO IN UMIDO PROFUMATO ALLA MENTA

LAMB FRICASSEE SCENTED WITH MINT

THIS FRICASSEE MAY be made with other cuts of lamb, such as the shoulder, breast, or rump. This dish is very simple, but quite often the less refined a dish is, the more flavorful it is.

SERVES 6

3 lb lamb leg, cleaned

3 tbsp olive oil

4 garlic cloves, peeled and crushed

2 fresh bay leaves

2 rosemary sprigs

2 tbsp all-purpose white flour

Salt and freshly ground black pepper, as needed

1½ cups dry white wine

1 cup Brodo (page 49) or low-sodium meat or chicken broth, plus as needed

3 large eggs, lightly beaten

¼ cup freshly squeezed lemon juice

1 tbsp chopped fresh flat-leaf parsley

1 tbsp chopped fresh mint leaves

1. Trim the excess fat from the lamb; cut the meat into pieces about the size of a small egg.

2. In a casserole, warm the oil with the crushed garlic over low heat. When the garlic is lightly browned, about 1 minute, add the lamb pieces, bay leaves, and rosemary. Sauté over high heat until the lamb is lightly colored all over, about 5 minutes. Stir in the flour a little at a time. When it begins to become a little brown, about 3 minutes, season with salt and pepper to taste, and pour in the wine. Simmer over medium heat until the alcohol evaporates, about 5 minutes. Add the broth and lower the heat. Cover and cook gently until the meat is very tender, about 35 to 40 minutes, adding a little more broth if necessary. The sauce should be quite thin in consistency. Remove from the heat.

3. Remove the meat to a separate dish. In a bowl, beat the eggs with the lemon juice. Stir in the egg and lemon mixture, combining it well with the pan juices, until a creamy sauce is formed. Return the meat to the sauce, add the parsley and mint, and serve at once.

||||||||||||||||||||||
WINE SUGGESTION

White: Verdicchio | Red: Aglianico

Arrotolata di Vitello alla Lucana

Roasted Veal Roll in the Style of Lucania

THE SOUTHERN ITALIAN region of Basilicata was the site of the ancient district of Lucania, for which this dish is named. For the best results, make sure that once the meat starts simmering, you keep the heat very, very low. Serve this with a big red wine, like a Barolo or a Negro Amaro.

SERVES 6

1 cup shredded spinach or Swiss chard leaves

1 garlic clove, chopped

1 tbsp chopped fresh oregano

2 tbsp chopped fresh parsley

½ cup freshly grated Pecorino Romano D.O.P

¼ cup golden raisins, plumped in Marsala

Zest of half a lemon

4 hard-cooked large eggs, peeled and coarsely chopped

¼ cup coarsely chopped almonds

Fresh hot pepper, as needed

Salt and freshly ground pepper, as needed

1½ pounds veal breast, butterflied and pounded thin

¼ cup extra-virgin olive oil

1 medium onion, chopped

1 celery stalk, thinly sliced

1 carrot, thinly sliced

1 fresh bay leaf

2 cups dry white wine

1 lb canned plum tomatoes, preferably imported San Marzano, crushed, with juices

1. To make the filling, combine the spinach or Swiss chard, garlic, herbs, cheese, raisins, lemon zest, hard boiled eggs, almonds, and hot pepper in a large bowl. Season with salt and pepper.

2. Spread the veal breast flat on a work surface and evenly spread the filling over the veal. Roll the veal breast over the filling in jelly-roll fashion, making sure to keep it tight (as if you were making a wrap). Tie it up securely with butcher twine to prevent the filling from leaking.

3. In an ovenproof sauté pan large enough to hold the veal, heat the oil over medium-high heat, and brown the veal on all sides. Remove the veal from the pan and set aside.

4. In the same pan, add the onion, celery, carrot, and bay leaf, and cook until they begin to take on color, about 5 to 6 minutes. Pour in the wine and allow the alcohol to evaporate, about 3 minutes. Stir in the tomatoes and return the veal to the pan. Bring the pan liquid to a simmer and cook over the lowest possible heat, covered, until the meat is very tender, 1 to 1½ hours. (Alternatively, once the liquid comes to a simmer, transfer the pan to a 300°F oven to finish cooking, about 1½ hours.) Add additional water or broth as needed to keep the veal moist.

5. Remove the meat from the pan and transfer it to a carving board. Use kitchen shears to carefully snip off the twine, then slice the veal into servings. Adjust the seasoning of the sauce with additional salt and pepper, if needed, and serve along with the slices of veal.

Peposo di Manzo con la Zucca

Peppery Beef Stew with Butternut Squash

THIS FLAVORFUL BEEF STEW comes from Tuscany, where it's ideal with the region's famed red wines. *Guanciale* is cured pork jowl, which you can find in some Italian specialty markets. Pancetta makes an acceptable substitute.

SERVES 6 TO 8

4 oz guanciale or pancetta

8 oz cipollini or pearl onions

3 lb beef chuck-eye roast, cut into
    1½ inch-cubes

1½ tsp kosher or sea salt

2 tsp coarsely ground black pepper

All-purpose flour, as needed

2 cups coarsely chopped onion

½ cup chopped celery

3 garlic cloves, peeled and crushed

¼ cup all-purpose flour

2 cups full-bodied dry red wine

2 tbsp dried porcini mushrooms, reconstituted and finely chopped

1 cup Brodo (page 49) or low-sodium meat
    or chicken broth

2 fresh bay leaves

1 sprig fresh rosemary, leaves only,
    finely chopped

2 sprigs fresh thyme, leaves only,
    finely chopped

½ lb white mushrooms, brushed clean
    and quartered

2 cups cubed butternut squash or pumpkin,
    peeled and seeded

2 tbsp fresh chopped flat-leaf parsley

(recipe continues on page 146)

1. In an ample ovensafe Dutch oven over medium heat, sauté the guanciale or pancetta until it is browned, about 6 minutes. Remove from the pan using a slotted spoon and spread it out on a paper towel. Reserve the drippings for use later.

2. Bring a pot of water to a rapid boil over high heat. Peel and trim the onions lightly (but try not to cut the root end too deep; that will help the onion hold together as it cooks.) Add the cipollini or pearl onions to the water and cook at a boil until the tip of a paring knife slides about halfway into the onion, about 6 to 7 minutes. Drain and set aside.

3. Preheat the oven to 300°F.

4. Place the beef cubes in large bowl. Season with salt and pepper to taste. Pile the flour onto a piece of waxed paper or place it in a flat plate. Dredge the meat in the flour, shaking off any excess. Heat 2 tablespoons of the reserved pancetta fat or olive oil in the Dutch oven over medium-high heat. Add the beef in two separate batches.

5. Brown the meat on all sides, about 5 minutes, adding another tablespoon of fat, if needed. Remove the meat and set it aside. Add the chopped onion and celery to the pot and sauté until almost softened, 4 to 5 minutes. Reduce the heat and the add garlic. Continue to sauté for about 30 seconds more. Stir in the flour and, when it is lightly colored, about 2 minutes, pour in the wine. Add the porcini, scraping up any browned bits that may have stuck to pot. Add the broth, bay leaves, rosemary, thyme, and reserved pork bits and bring to simmer. Return the meat to the pan and bring the liquid to a simmer once again. Cover and slide the pot into the oven. Cook for a total of about 2 hours.

6. In the meantime, in an ample skillet, heat 2 tablespoons of the reserved pancetta drippings or olive oil over high heat until hot enough to sear the mushrooms. Add the white mushrooms and sauté until browned, tossing frequently, about 5 minutes. Remove the mushrooms from skillet using a slotted spoon and set them aside. Add the par-cooked cippolini or pearl onions and sauté over high heat until lightly browned, 2 to 3 minutes. Remove the pan from the heat and set aside.

7. When the meat starts getting tender, after about 1½ hours, add the butternut squash or pumpkin to the stew. Cover and return to the oven. Cook until the meat, squash, onions and celery are tender, about 20 to 30 minutes longer. Stir in the reserved mushrooms and the parsley, taste, and season with additional salt, if needed, and plenty of pepper.

‖‖‖‖‖‖‖‖‖‖‖‖
RECIPE NOTES

This peppery beef stew is usually served by itself, accompanied only by more freshly ground black pepper, but it would also be great to serve with some Naughty Polenta (page 86).

This dish can be made up to 4 days in advance and kept in an air-tight container in the refrigerator.

‖‖‖‖‖‖‖‖‖‖‖‖‖‖‖
WINE SUGGESTION

Chianti Riserva or Brunello

ZUCCHINE ALLE ERBETTE

ZUCCHINI WITH FRESH HERBS

WHEN YOU BUY zucchini, look for firm, small- to medium-sized zucchini; avoid very large ones. In some parts of Italy, this dish is also called *in scapece*, which indicates some kind of sweet/sour marinade. You can make eggplant in this way, as well as endive, carrots, or *radicchio di Treviso*. Serve this dish in the summer by itself or as an accompaniment for almost any grilled dish.

SERVES 6

2 lb medium zucchini, 6 to 8 oz each

Kosher salt, as needed

⅔ cup extra-virgin olive oil, as needed for frying

All-purpose flour, as needed

1 cup very thinly sliced red onion

Fresh chile pepper or hot red pepper flakes, as needed

4 garlic cloves, thinly sliced

2 tbsp chopped fresh mint

2 tbsp chopped fresh flat-leaf parsley

1 tbsp chopped fresh basil

¾ cup white wine vinegar

¼ cup sugar

1. Cut off the stem and tip ends of the zucchini and slice them ⅓ inch thick on the bias. Sprinkle liberally with salt and place them in a colander to drain for 1 hour. Rinse well, drain, and blot dry with paper toweling. While the zucchini is draining, line a plate with several layers of paper toweling to blot the zucchini after you fry it.

2. Heat a skillet over medium-high heat and add enough oil to come to a depth of ¼ inch. When the surface of the oil is hazy and appears to shimmer, it is hot enough to fry the zucchini.

3. Dredge the zucchini slices lightly in flour and shake off any excess. Immediately slip the zucchini slices into the hot oil, being careful not to splash the oil, and fry until golden on each side, 2 to 3 minutes. (You will have to do this in batches to avoid crowding the pan.) Remove them when cooked, drain on paper towels, and then transfer to a serving dish.

4. Heat 1 tablespoon of oil in a small sauté pan over medium-high heat. Add the onion slices and sauté, stirring frequently, until they are translucent but not colored, about 3 to 4 minutes. Stir in the chile pepper or pepper flakes, garlic, mint, parsley, basil, vinegar, and sugar and bring to a boil. Immediately pour this mixture over the fried zucchini. Cover the dish and let the zucchini marinate in the refrigerator for at least 6 hours before serving.

Fagioli al Fiasco "Rivisitati"

White Beans Cooked in a Flask "Revisited"

THE ORIGINAL RECIPE would require a flask, filled a little less than halfway with beans, then water up to almost the very top of the neck, some herbs, and some olive oil. The flask would be placed close to a heat source that was just hot enough to start the mixture simmering, next to an open fire for instance. Cooking them on top of the stove is not nearly as rustic, but will taste just as good, I promise.

SERVES 6

1 lb dry white beans	1 fresh bay leaf	Salt, as needed
5 fresh sage leaves	2 parsley stems	1 tbsp extra-virgin olive oil
3 garlic cloves, peeled and crushed	2 rosemary sprigs	

1. Before you soak the beans, make sure you spread them out on a flat surface or sheet pan and check for impurities. (At times there may be little stones, which could really ruin the recipe.) If you are using a flask, make sure the flask is big enough to hold all the beans.

2. Let the beans soak overnight in water, then wash them and cook them slowly in an appropriate pot beginning with cold water (covering the beans by about 2 to 3 inches).

3. Wrap the herbs in a piece of cheesecloth or tie them together with butcher twine to make a sachet, and add them to the beans. Bring the water with the beans and herbs to a simmer over low heat and cover. During the first 20 minutes of the simmering, skim the foam that might come on surface, and let cook through until tender, about 45 minutes to 1 hour, depending on the beans. Once cooked, remove the herbs and add salt as needed. The beans can be held in the refrigerator directly in the cooking liquid for 2 or 3 days. Drain the beans before using them in another dish, but try to reserve the bean cooking liquid to add to soups or stews.

Fritto Misto

Mixed Fry

THERE ARE MANY ways of frying food all over Italy, varying slightly depending upon the temperature of the oil, the type of oil that is used, the use of flour only as a coating, or first applying some sort of liquid (milk, water, cream) and then the flour, the addition of herbs (or not) and so on. Here I use a version that might not be strictly "Italian," but *is* quite easy and gives you great results. Remember it's only food and you are, at all times, supposed to have fun!

SERVES 6

2 qt peanut or olive oil, as needed

2 cups buttermilk or milk

1½ lb assorted vegetables, washed, dried, cut into bite-size pieces

2 cups all-purpose flour, as needed for breading (or a 50-50 blend of all-purpose and semolina flour for a crunchier texture)

1 tbsp paprika (optional)

Salt and freshly ground black pepper, as needed

1. Heat the oil to 375°F in a deep pot or fryer.

2. Place the buttermilk or milk in a shallow pan. In a separate pan, mix the flour and semolina with paprika, if using. Soak a few pieces of the prepared vegetables in the liquid at a time, then transfer to the flour mixture. Make sure the pieces get well coated. Do not flour the food and leave it to rest for too long; it will get too sticky and hard to handle, also the results will not be good. Shake off any excess flour and place into the hot oil.

3. Be sure that before you start frying, you have a pan lined with paper towels in which to drain the vegetables once cooked. Do not overcrowd the fryer; work in small batches, letting the oil "recuperate" and come back to temperature after each batch. Be sure to monitor the temperature of the oil during cooking.

4. Once the vegetables have been dropped into the hot oil, do not disturb them until they start getting some color, 1 to 2 minutes, depending on the size of the pieces. Once cooked, do not handle the vegetables too much or the breading will come off, and the vegetables will get greasy and limp. Season with salt and pepper and serve while hot.

||||||||||||||||
RECIPE NOTES

Calculate 1½ pounds of vegetables for 6 people, a little bit more if you are serving these as an accompaniment to fish or meat.

Peanut oil would be my first choice for frying, but olive oil also works well; it has a stronger, more aggressive flavor, but, of course, it is also more expensive.

PEPERONATA POVERA E PIGRA

"POOR AND LAZY" STEWED PEPPERS

I CALL THIS dish "poor and lazy," because there aren't too many ingredients or steps, and you can make a lot of it at once with no extra work. You will be surprised at how many ways you will use it—in pasta, served on a piece of bread, cold with slices of fresh mozzarella, or as a side with a grilled piece of fish or meat. Make sure you cook it completely—do not serve it crunchy; the whole flavor depends on achieving a tender texture. Add some hot pepper or garlic, if you like your food spicy. Olives, capers, raisins, legumes, or nuts may also be added at the very end.

SERVES 4

4 green bell peppers	½ cup chopped fresh flat-leaf parsley
2 red bell peppers	1 fresh bay leaf
2 yellow bell peppers	1 cup chopped tomatoes, fresh or canned, peeled and seeded
2½ cups extra-virgin olive oil, plus as needed for drizzling	Salt and freshly ground black pepper, as needed
3 red onions, sliced thin	
2 carrots, sliced ¼ inch thick	2 tbsp chopped basil leaves
4 celery stalks, trimmed, sliced ¼ inch thick	1 tbsp chopped oregano leaves

1. Wash the peppers, cut them in half, and remove the cores and stems. Cut them into large pieces and set aside.

2. In an ample pan with a cover, warm the olive oil. Add the onions and sauté over low heat until they are very soft, about 5 minutes. Stir in the carrots and celery and cook slowly until tender, another 5 minutes.

3. Add the peppers, ¼ cup of the parsley, and the bay leaf and stir for about 5 minutes to marry the flavors. Add the chopped tomatoes and season with salt and pepper. Cover and continue to cook over very low heat until the peppers are soft, about 45 minutes. Mix in the basil, oregano, and the rest of the parsley. If desired, drizzle with additional olive oil at the table.

Tortino di Carciofi alla Maggiorana

Artichoke and Egg Tortino

YOU CAN USE practically any ingredient you like to make a *tortino* following this recipe—asparagus, peas, chicory or any wild greens, peppers, sausage, onion, cheeses, and so on. Cook the tortino in a non-stick pie pan or a cast-iron skillet.

SERVES 4

4 medium artichokes, cleaned (see note below)

2 tbsp extra-virgin olive oil, plus additional for oiling pan

½ cup minced shallots or onions

2 tbsp chopped fresh flat-leaf parsley

½ cup dry white wine

8 large eggs

½ cup freshly grated Parmigiano-Reggiano cheese

2 tbsp fresh marjoram, coarsely chopped

Salt and freshly ground black pepper, as needed

1. Cut the artichokes into thin slices, slicing from top to bottom. The slices will separate into rings, a little like the way onion slices separate.

2. Warm the olive oil in a saucepan. Add the shallots and sauté over medium-high heat until translucent, about 2 minutes. Stir in the parsley, followed by the artichokes. Cook for 2 minutes. Add the wine, cover, and cook to evaporate the alcohol and steam the artichokes. When the artichokes are tender, about 12 min-

utes, remove the pan from the heat and allow to cool somewhat.

3. Preheat an oven to 325°F. Oil an 8-inch pie pan or cast-iron skillet.

4. In a medium bowl, beat the eggs with the grated cheese, marjoram, salt, and pepper. Add the artichokes and mix until combined. Pour the egg mixture into the pan and slide it into the oven. Bake until the eggs are completely set, about 12 minutes.

CLEANING ARTICHOKES

The way you plan to serve artichokes determines what steps need to be followed to prepare them. Fill a bowl with a mixture of water and lemon juice to hold artichokes after they are cut. Whole artichokes for stuffing or serving with a dip need to be trimmed of sharp barbs; kitchen scissors are the best tool for this task. Spread open the leaves and scoop out the purple tipped leaves and hairy filaments with a spoon. For artichoke hearts, cut away most of the tough outer leaves, making sure that you keep "caressing" the outer part with a halved lemon, which will keep the artichokes from turning black. Leave only the base and tender inner leaves behind. To make an artichoke bottom, cut the leaves completely away from the base of the artichoke.

"*L'uva cattiva non fa buon vino.*"

Bad grapes don't make good wine.

— ITALIAN PROVERB

THE ITALIAN APPROACH TO WINE

EVER SINCE THE time I was a young child, I can only recall two beverages that were consistently served at our dinner table: water and wine. My mother felt that milk and juices were to be enjoyed with breakfast or as a refreshment at other moments of the day, but not at the dinner table. We always had to earn the little glass of Coke that was very rarely to be found in our refrigerator.

While water was the main beverage for young children, in our culture it was normal for children to begin to experience wine with their food at a very tender age. This may sound odd to an American reader, but I think I may have been only eight years old when I first tasted wine. At the dinner table, I always sat between my *nonna* and *nonno*—my grandparents. Nonna would mix a little wine with some water, and when she gave it to me, would always recite, "*Acqua e vino fa bene ai bambini.*" (Water and wine is good for children.)

Italians tend to take a different approach to drinking than Americans. Wine is something your family educates you about, teaching you in words and in actions to properly appreciate this wonderful beverage. Being exposed to wine in that environment has given me several advantages. Not only did I learn how to responsibly enjoy drinking alcoholic beverages in general and how to confidently pair wines with food, but I also gained a lifelong passion that is both avocation and profession, an enthusiasm for which I am delighted to share with others.

Wine is an everyday affair for Italians. You may have heard that the typical Italian person has between four and six glasses of wine a day. That is true. What keeps this fact from being a matter of grave national concern is both the kind of wine being drunk and the fact that wine is rarely a beverage drunk by itself. Italians understand that wine is a beverage to be appreciated with food. It will enhance the flavor of your dishes and make you feel good. Enjoyed as the typical Italian does, it's definitely good for your body, and your soul.

For the most part, Italians favor what we call *vino sfuso* or *vino da tavola* (table wine) to drink with daily meals, at both lunch and dinner. This is a wine made by local farmers that does not typically have any appellation; it is produced in large quantities and is not put in labeled bottles. *Vino sfuso* or *da tavola* is usually 5 to 7% alcohol by volume. Compare that to the alcohol content of a typical "bottled" wine at 11 to 15%. For Italians, these bottled wines are reserved for special occasions, and are not consumed as a daily beverage. If you replace those six glasses of a typical Italian table wine

with the same amount of a typical bottled wine, you'd probably be drunk all day!

For a traditional Italian household, buying wine holds its own rituals and traditions. It is one of my great memories of growing up in Italy. We were not snobby about wine, and spending outrageous amounts of money on it was unthinkable. We had "connections"—family members and friends were always our providers. The wine was put in a big cask and then, once we got the cask home, poured into our own glass bottles that were stored in a pantry outside on our balcony.

Pairing food and wine is easy enough. Here's one thing to remember about Italian wines and wines in general: Don't be intimidated. There are some tried and true standards that I have used to make the wine recommendations that accompany some of the recipes in this book. As you might imagine, there are traditional pairings of food and wine that are widely observed. As you experience more wines, you will gain an instinct for selecting a good wine for any meal, even when your favorite labels aren't on the store shelf or wine list.

To become truly expert at pairing food and wine is to take on a lifelong challenge, one that I find to be compelling and most enjoyable. You try to strike a balance between the flavors of the wine and the food. There is a subtle interplay in which the flavors of the wine enhance and accentuate those of the food and vice versa. The wine is a true supporting player. Perhaps even more challenging is matching wine and food so that a contrast is created. This effect differentiates the flavors rather than marrying with them.

An excellent way to get to know wine is to taste new wines often and keep notes on your impressions. Some people like to remove the wine labels from new or special bottles (there are various kits available to assist in removing the label from the bottle without damage) and collect them in a wine notebook, along with their general impressions of the color, flavor, and finish of the wine, as well as what foods were enjoyed with the bottle. You can find wine tasting journals in many bookstores or online. Take every opportunity to expose yourself to new wines, perhaps by attending local wine tastings, or taking a course to learn more about different styles of wine and wine making in general. The more you expose yourself to different wines, the more confident you will become in making your own selections.

Part of being able to enjoy food and wine together is having wine on hand. You don't have to fill a whole wine cellar to be prepared; a wine rack with a few essentials is fine. What should you choose to fill your rack? Italy has over 300 grape varietals and stocking your wine rack with every single one of them will be pretty much impossible. Use the following guidelines to make sure you have the basics at the ready:

Red wines are certainly the pride and joy of my country. As we say, "Il vino è rosso." (The wine is red.) At their best, our reds offer a taste of the sun and soil that created them. The taste is robust, direct, and earthy, with an elegant finish—a perfect companion for the bold flavors so much a part of Italian cooking.

A bottle of *Sangiovese* (the most planted grape varietal in Tuscany, and the principle grape in such well known wines as Chianti and Brunello di Montalcino) would never go wrong with a pasta dish or even a pizza. Despite a popular misconception that it is a "cheap" wine, Chianti is, in reality, one of the more elegant and subtle wines, one that Italy is justifiably proud of. However, you may remember trying a poor-quality "Chianti" served in the ubiquitous rush-covered bottle, known as a *fiasco*—the Italian word for flask, but the English meaning of that word may have strengthened the impression that the wine was not very good. However the quality of contemporary Italian wines is now very strictly controlled and consistently excellent.

The *Nebbiolo* grapes grown in Piedmont region in northern Italy produce heavier reds like the well-known Barolo, with a good level of tannins that are a wonderful complement to intensely flavored braises and ragus. Simpler Nebbiolo-based wines may be referred to as a *Barolo bambino* (baby Barolo). Wines made from the *Aglianico* grape, which originated in Greece, are an excellent match for lamb and game dishes. *Primitivo* (one of the oldest grapes still produced) is a young, vibrant red that is best paired with the spicy dishes of southern Italy. *Valpolicella* and *Dolcetto* are good wines to keep on hand if you enjoy lighter reds to pair with white meats or fish.

Sparkling wines are wonderful before the meal has begun; the acidity cleanses your palate and gets you ready to receive your food. When I go to a restaurant, I always start with a glass of sparkling wine and look at the menu as I sip it. By the time I'm ready to order, every single thing on the menu looks so appetizing, all because the wine has teased my palette and increased my appetite. For an Italian sparkling wine, I definitely recommend you sample a few different Proseccos to find your own "house favorite."

If you enjoy whites wines that have high acidity with a crisp finish, you definitely want to experience the wines from the Northern side of Italy; for something that has more of a tropical finish with a hint of earthiness, wines from the South. The old soil and volcanic conditions plus the method of making white wines in Italy result in wines with acidity as the predominant flavor. So if you are used to a typical California buttery, vanilla flavor and lots of oak chardonnay, don't look for it, because you won't be able to find it.

Pinot Grigio is arguably the most popular white wine made in Italy. *Trebbiano* is the third most planted grape in Italy. Other important wine varieties are Tocai, Verdicchio and Falanghina (which translates as "the happy one"). These are wines that will work with cold appetizers, salads, some pasta in a light oil-and-garlic sauce, or a fish entrée.

Don't forget about a dessert wine to serve with the final course. *Moscato d'Asti* is always popular for any dessert because of its fruity characteristics, and the Bracchetto is an ideal pairing to enjoy with chocolate.

CHAPTER FIVE

DIGESTIVI, LIQUORI E DOLCI

Digestives, Liqueurs, and Desserts

Cappolino

Basil Liqueur

MY SISTER, CATERINA, always says you should not try making a digestive unless the herbs you plan to use are in season, or it won't taste like it's supposed to. I remember going to her house in the summer, when basil was at its peak season. Having come from a full lunch at our mother's house, Caterina offered me a shot of this homemade liqueur, saying it would help my digestion. Well, a few minutes later, I felt great—all I wanted to do was take a good afternoon nap under her fig tree!

MAKES 1¾ QUARTS

40 fresh basil leaves

Zest of 2 organic lemons

3 cups grain alcohol

4 cups water

3 cups sugar

1. Wash the basil in cool water and blot it dry with a cloth. Place in a large bowl.

2. Add the lemon zest and grain alcohol to the bowl and let the mixture marry, covered, for 24 hours at room temperature.

3. In a large pot, bring the water to a boil over high heat, add the sugar, and stir until the sugar dissolves. Remove from the heat.

4. Allow the water to cool, then add it to the basil-zest-alcohol mixture, and pour it into a large jar with a lid. Let it rest in a cool, dark cupboard for about 20 days

5. Double strain through cheesecloth and then pour it into clean bottles. Cap the bottles tightly. Keep refrigerated after the liqueur bottled. It is appreciated when served very cold.

Digestivo dei Quattro Gatti

Orange-Coffee Digestive

MY SISTERS WERE given this recipe by Marcella, an elderly friend of theirs in Vicenza. They modified it a bit, because they thought the original recipe was perhaps too strong for people not accustomed to strong digestives. You can use an inexpensive grappa for this, no need for something more pricey.

MAKES 3 PINTS

1 bottle (750 ml) unflavored grappa

½ cup sugar

½ vanilla bean (about 2 inches long), split but not scraped

1 navel orange

44 coffee beans

1. In a glass jar with an opening large enough to fit the orange, pour in the grappa and sugar and shake well. Add the vanilla bean.

2. Using a small knife, make 44 small cuts in the orange skin, large enough to accommodate the coffee beans. Insert the beans in the slits, avoiding penetrating the skin and actually touching the flesh of the orange segments.

3. Add the orange to the grappa-sugar mixture and let it rest, covered, for 44 days in a cool

and completely dark place. On the final day, lift out the orange and vanilla bean and discard. Filter the remaining liquid through clean cheesecloth into a sterilized receptacle. The digestive will be amber-orange from the fruit. Serve cold or at room temperature, as you like.

Liquore alla Liquerizia di Livio

Livio's Licorice Liqueur

LIVIO HAS BEEN a good friend of mine since we were teenagers. Since moving to America, I only see him when I return home to visit my family, but when we get together, we eat enough to make up for any lost time—Livio is a great cook, and in true Italian fashion, he won't let you say no to extra helpings. The last memorable drink we had together (after several different wines) was this superb licorice liqueur with a powerful, sweet zing.

MAKES 3 PINTS

2 fresh 4-inch licorice root sticks

12 to 15 (or to taste) olive-sized genuine Italian licorice candies, such as Panda brand

1 bottle (750 ml) unflavored grappa

1. Break and slightly smash the licorice root sticks. In a bowl, combine them with the licorice candies and the grappa, cover the bowl, and allow them to soak on a sunny windowsill for about 30 days, shaking every 5 days or so.

2. After the initial soaking period of about 30 days, let it rest for another month away from the sun, undisturbed. It should not be shaken during this second soaking period.

3. After the second 30 days, pass the alcohol mixture through a double layer of clean cheesecloth. Transfer it to a sterilized bottle and cap it. Serve cold or at room temperature.

||||||||||||

VARIATION:

This can be made successfully substituting vodka in place of the grappa. I tried making this with a vanilla vodka with nice results.

Digestivo della Casa

The "House" Digestive

IF YOU SPEND any length of time in Italy, it won't be long before you notice people telling one another, "have this, it will help you digest," or "have that, it will increase your appetite." There are endless variations on the herbal digestive theme all over Italy—each family has its own version. Here is one from mine.

MAKES 1 QUART

1 qt grappa, 40 proof

½ cup sugar

20 fresh sage leaves

1 sprig fresh rosemary

4 to 6 spearmint leaves

Mix all the ingredients together and let rest, covered, in a cool dark place for 40 to 50 days, then filter into clean bottles. Cap the bottles tightly and store them in a dark cupboard or liquor cabinet.

Lo Sgroppino

Prosecco-Lemon-Vodka Digestive

IN EVERY SMALL trattoria or pizzeria in the Veneto, you will find this typical digestive being offered as an after-dinner drink, particularly in the summer, when it makes the perfect end to a meal. It is easy to make and impressive if presented in a beautiful flute with some kind of garnish—candied lemon rind, a mint leaf, or even a few raspberries or blueberries.

SERVES 4 TO 5

1½ cups lemon sorbet

¼ cup vodka

⅓ cup prosecco, chilled

1. In a blender, mix the sorbet and vodka for a few seconds. Add the prosecco and pulse for a few more seconds, just until the mixture is thoroughly blended and smooth. If the drink looks separated, you can add a tablespoon of milk to "emulsify" the drink.

2. Divide the *sgroppino* among 4 or 5 champagne flutes or dessert goblets and serve at once.

Nocillo

Fresh Walnut Liqueur

It is said that you must pick the walnuts on the Feast of San Giuseppe (March 19), when they are still green. If you don't, the chance that the liqueur will go bad is very high. Or perhaps not, but it is a tradition, so I wouldn't mess with it.

MAKES 1 ¾ QUARTS

30 fresh peeled walnuts

1 tbsp ground cinnamon

6 cloves

2¾ cups sugar, divided

3 cups grain alcohol

4 cups water

1. Peel the walnuts and cut them into tiny pieces. In a glass container that has a cover, add the walnut pieces, cinnamon, cloves, 1 cup sugar, and the grain alcohol. Cover the container and leave it in a sunny area for 20 days, making sure to shake it on a daily basis.

2. After 20 days, combine 1¾ cups sugar and the 4 cups water in a saucepan. Cook over medium heat, stirring constantly, until the liquid becomes clear. Do not allow the syrup to reach the boiling point. Turn off the heat and allow to cool to room temperature. Add this syrup to the alcohol and allow to rest overnight.

3. Double or triple strain the mixture and pour into clean bottles. Cap the bottles tightly and store in a dark cupboard. Nocillo should be appreciated at room temperature.

PAGE 165 AND THIS PAGE, CLOCKWISE FROM TOP:
Cappolino, Digestivo dei 44 Gatti, Liquore alla Liquerizia di Livio, Lo Sgroppino, Nocillo

LIMONCELLO

LEMON RIND LIQUEUR

THE AMALFI COAST, rising high above the crystal blue Mediterranean Sea, is without a doubt one of the most beautiful places in Italy. This stunning landscape has been the inspiration of musicians, writers, and poets for hundreds of years. Just the mention of the towns of Amalfi, Positano, Sorrento, Vietri, Ravello (my favorite), and the island of Capri conjures images of an earthly paradise to people all over the world. In this land grow the huge lemons used for the region's famous *limoncello*. It is a digestive that needs to be appreciated after a meal. Because it is very viscous and intensely flavored, it should be served in a tiny-stemmed glass and sipped little by little to ensure that it goes down slowly and gently. In this way, its clear and crisp lemon scent will unfold instead of overpower. What a wonderful way to end a Sunday dinner. Limoncello should be kept in the freezer after it is made; because of its high alcohol content, it will not freeze.

MAKES 1¾ QUARTS

12 lemons (preferably Meyer)

3 cups grain alcohol

4 cups water

2½ cups sugar

1. Carefully wash the lemons in cold water to prevent bruising them. With a very sharp, small knife, cut off the yellow rind in a spiral fashion, making sure not to remove any of the white pith beneath, which could impart an unpleasant bitter flavor to the drink.

2. Put the zests into a sterilized glass container and pour the alcohol over them. Seal the container and store in a cool, dark place for 36 to 40 days, making sure to shake the mixture at least once a day. The liquid should be almost white at the end of the process.

3. In a saucepan, combine the water and sugar and cook over medium heat, stirring constantly, until the liquid becomes clear. Do not allow the syrup to reach the boiling point. Turn off the heat and allow it to cool to room temperature.

4. Pour the syrup into the container with the alcohol and rind (it will have lost most of its yellow color at this point, and may be discarded). Stir everything together, reseal the container, and leave it to stand an additional 7 days.

5. Double strain the liqueur using a double layer of cheesecloth. Transfer to a clean bottle, seal, and put in the freezer. Serve cold, directly from the freezer.

Biscottini al Vino Dolce

Small Cookies with Sweet Wine

SERVE THESE DELICIOUS cookies, which contain raisins soaked in a sweet dessert wine like Vin Santo or Marsala, along with chilled glasses of the same wine to dip the cookies into. You could also try them with an ice cold glass of limoncello (page 169).

MAKES 3½ DOZEN BISCOTTINI

⅓ cup golden raisins

¾ cup sweet wine such as Vin Santo or Marsala

3⅔ cups all-purpose flour

½ cup sugar

3 oz semi-sweet chocolate, coarsely chopped

½ cup pine nuts

¾ cup canola oil or a very mild olive oil

½ tsp vanilla extract

Pinch of ground cinnamon

1 tsp baking powder

Pinch of salt

Powdered sugar, for dusting

1. Soak the raisins in the sweet wine for at least 1 hour, then drain off any liquid that the raisins haven't absorbed.

2. Preheat the oven to 325°F.

3. Use a food processor to combine all of the ingredients (except the powdered sugar) just enough to form a mass of dough. Form into little balls, about the size of a large marble, and lightly flatten the tops. Place them 1½ inches apart on a cookie sheet or baking pan lined with parchment paper, and bake them for 12 to 15 minutes, or until lightly browned. Remove them to racks and let them cool. Lightly dust the tops of the biscottini with powdered sugar before serving.

Dolcetti Ripieni di Fichi

Small Fig Cookies

THIS IS A very old recipe from my Aunt Angela. Everything she used to make was *"a occhio,"* which means "by the eyes"—a little bit of this, a little bit of that. It took me a while to figure out her particular proportions for this recipe, but I think I've come quite close.

MAKES ABOUT 30 COOKIES

2 cups all-purpose flour

¼ cup whole wheat flour

½ cup sugar

Pinch of salt

1 tsp lemon or orange zest

1¾ sticks (14 tbsp) unsalted butter, cut into large cubes, at room temperature

1 large egg

1 large egg yolk

1 tsp rum

1 tsp vanilla extract

FIG FILLING

1½ cups dry figs, try the ones with as
    few seeds as possible

½ cup golden raisins, soaked
    in Marsala

1 cup pitted dates

¼ cup chopped toasted walnuts

¼ cup shelled pistachios, toasted

¼ cup fresh orange juice

½ tsp allspice

2 tbsp water

2 tbsp Grand Marnier or Cointreau

Egg wash (made from 1 egg beaten
    with 2 tbsp milk)

Powdered sugar, for dusting

1. *For the dough*: Mix the two flours together with the sugar, salt, and the lemon or orange zest. Cut in the butter using two knives or a pastry knife without working it too much. Use your hands to mix until the dough resembles sand. Add the egg, yolk, rum, and vanilla; mix until it comes together. Do not overwork it. Wrap in plastic wrap and set aside to rest in the refrigerator until ready to use.

2. *For the filling*: Mix all the ingredients, except the liquor, together and chop in a food processor until the mixture is a little bit coarse, but not too thin. Put the mixture into a saucepan and cook very slowly over low heat until it thickens, about 6 minutes. Remove from the heat and stir in the liquor. Cover and refrigerate until chilled.

3. Preheat the oven to 350°F and line a baking sheet with parchment paper.

4. Divide the dough into thirds. On a floured surface roll each third of dough into a rectangular shape about 5 inches wide, 10 inches long, and ¼ inch thick. Spoon a third of the filling down the center of each rectangle. Fold the dough over the filling as if you were making a strudel. Pinch the ends together to seal and place, sealed side down, on the prepared pan. Brush the top and sides with the egg wash. Repeat with the remaining dough and filling.

5. Bake for about 20 minutes, until the tops are lightly browned. Remove and let cool on a wire rack. Slice the logs to make 1 inch cookies. Once they are completely cooled, dust the tops with powdered sugar and serve.

〰〰〰〰〰〰
RECIPE NOTE

You can make the filling in advance if you'd like. It freezes well.

Another way to make this recipe is to slice the logs into cookies before you bake them. Place the cookies seam side down on a prepared baking sheet. Bake for about 15 to 20 minutes, until the tops are golden brown.

BICERINO DI CIOCCOLATO ALLA NOCCIOLA

HAZELNUT HOT CHOCOLATE

THIS IS A variation of the typical hot chocolate you'll find in pretty much any bar in Italy during the cold months. It is usually very dense and super hot, made with steamed milk like a cappuccino. I can remember when I was a child, Sunday afternoons in the wintertime, all the ladies would gather at the bar in the village after church to have hot chocolate with whipped cream, while the men would have a little *ombretta* (a small glass of wine) or an aperitif a couple of hours before lunch. Choose a good chocolate—one that contains 60% or higher cocoa butter—for a very rich taste. This recipe will give you about four 6-ounce cups of hot chocolate, depending on how well you press the hazelnuts. Sugar is an adjustable ingredient, depending on the quality and the kind of chocolate you are using.

SERVES 4

½ cup hazelnuts, whole, skin on

4 cups whole milk, cold

¼ cup Dutch processed cocoa powder, European-style

2 tbsp powdered sugar, or as needed

10 oz semi-sweet chocolate, grated

½ cup heavy cream, whipped into stiff peaks, for topping

1. Preheat the oven to 300°F. Toast the hazelnuts in the oven until lightly brown, about 10 to 15 minutes, being careful not to let them burn. Once toasted, place them on a towel and rub well to remove the skins. Grind in a food processor until evenly ground but not floury; reserve.

2. In a saucepan, stir together the cold milk, cocoa powder, and sugar and bring to a simmer over low heat; make sure there aren't any lumps. Remove from the heat and pour into the bowl with the ground hazelnuts. Let steep for at least 1 hour, until cool. You may do this the day before and let the mixture rest in the refrigerator.

3. Strain the milk-hazelnut-cocoa mixture through a fine mesh sieve into a saucepan, making sure you press the hazelnuts well to release the flavor. Heat the milk until it is warm, but not boiling, over low heat, remove from the heat, add the grated chocolate, and mix well until the chocolate is melted. When ready to serve, reheat the hot chocolate and serve immediately with a dollop of whipped cream.

||||||||||||||||||||

RECIPE NOTES

Try adding a pinch of chili powder, cinnamon, or a tiny pinch of sea salt to the hot chocolate before serving. A little vanilla extract would be a nice addition as well. If you want to omit the step of steeping the toasted hazelnuts in the milk, you could use a chocolate like Valrhona Caraibe 60% Hazelnut or Gianduia, which will give you the same intense hazelnut flavor.

Frittelle con Ricotta

Ricotta Fritters

IF THE RICOTTA is very wet, be sure to drain it well before proceeding with the recipe, and adjust the amount of flour if necessary. If you can replace the baking powder with a single packet of Italian *lievito* for *dolci* (look for it in Italian specialty stores), you might just have the perfect recipe. My sister, Caterina, adds raisins soaked in Marsala or grappa to this recipe. She used to make these only for Carnivale in February, but since everybody likes them so much, she goes out of her way to make them more often.

SERVES 4 TO 6

8 oz fresh ricotta, drained

4 large eggs

6 tbsp sugar

1 tbsp dark rum

3 tbsp fresh orange juice

1 tsp baking powder

Pinch of salt

1 cup all-purpose flour, as needed

2 qt canola or peanut oil for frying

Powdered or granulated sugar, for dusting

1. Mix all ingredients except the flour together. Add the flour a little at a time as needed, until the dough is not too wet and it resembles a very wet bread dough.

2. Heat the oil to 350°F.

3. Using a teaspoon, carefully drop the fritters into the hot oil. It is best to work in batches and not overcrowd the pan. Let cook for 5 minutes, or until lightly brown.

4. Remove the fritters from the oil and let drain on paper towels. Dust with powdered or granulated sugar and serve hot.

Cremetta Fritta alla Veneziana

Venetian Cream Fritters

THESE SWEET CREAM FRITTERS are perfect to snack on while roaming the streets of town during Carnevale. I have fond memories of my Aunt Maria making these during those lazy, cold and rainy Februaries around the time of the carnival celebration, when all the kids used to dress up as different *personaggi* (characters). My favorite was Arlecchino (Harlequin), and my other aunt, Angela, would make me a new Arlecchino costume every year for our local school's costume contest.

SERVES 6

5 large eggs

1 cup sugar, plus as needed
   for dusting

1½ cups sifted all-purpose flour

Zest of 1 lemon

4 cups milk

½ tsp pure vanilla extract

Pinch of salt

2 cups plain bread crumbs

4 cups peanut oil, or as needed,
   for frying

1. Separate the egg yolks from the egg whites, reserving both.

2. In a heavy-bottomed saucepan, beat the egg yolks with the sugar until well combined. Add the flour and lemon zest, mixing constantly. Gradually add the milk and continue to mix until thoroughly combined. Add the vanilla and the salt; stir to blend.

3. Place the saucepan on low heat and gently cook, stirring continuously, until the mixture is creamy and hard—just before it boils. Pour the mixture out onto a cool, lightly oiled surface (marble or a baking sheet would work), and allow to cool completely.

4. Cut the cooled mixture into rectangles, rounds, or triangles, as you prefer. Beat the re-served egg whites to very soft peaks. Dip each rectangle in the egg whites and then in the bread crumbs.

5. Heat the oil to 350°F and fry each rectangle until golden, about 1 minute per side. Drain on paper towels, sprinkle some sugar on top, and serve warm.

||||||||||||||||||
RECIPE NOTES

You may add grappa or rum to the recipe if you want a more distinctive flavor. If you are serving children, try adding orange zest, cinnamon, or other "sweet" spices for a good non-alcoholic alternative. If you like chocolate, add some cocoa powder. Enjoy these fritters hot or at room temperature. If there are actually any leftovers, they can be enjoyed cold as well.

Bigoloni Integrali

Two-Flour Horseshoe Cookies

MY BROTHER, MARIO, and I would get into trouble every time we helped my mom make these cookies (okay, mostly me). The reason was that he, being four years younger than me, couldn't shape the cookies correctly (at least, in my opinion, he couldn't), which really frustrated me. I would tease him, and this would put me in bad stead with my mom, who would inevitably send me to my room before I got to make any of the cookies or, for that day, eat any, either. I would finally get to taste them the next day; of course, they were not as good-looking as the cookies I could have made (though truth be told, taste-wise, they were not so bad after all). You may substitute hazelnuts or pine nuts for the walnuts, if you wish. Serve the *bigoloni* with hot chocolate, some sweet wine, or a good Marsala.

MAKES ABOUT 2½ DOZEN COOKIES

1½ cups all-purpose flour

1¼ cups whole wheat flour

⅔ cup sugar

1 large egg white

¾ cup butter, unsalted, cubed
    and softened

Pinch of salt

Pinch of cinnamon

1 tsp vanilla extract

1 cup finely ground walnuts

Powdered sugar, for dusting

1. Sift the 2 flours together with the sugar and mound them on a work surface. Make a well in the center of the mound and add the egg white, cubed butter, salt, cinnamon, vanilla, and walnuts. Mix well, but do not overwork the dough. As soon as the dough comes together, cover with plastic wrap, and let rest in the refrigerator for at least 20 minutes.

2. Preheat the oven to 375°F.

3. Pinch a small amount of dough about the size of a large marble and, on a lightly floured surface, roll the dough to form a log that is a ½ inch thick and 2 inches long. Bend it slightly to give it the shape of a small horseshoe. Place the cookies on a buttered and floured baking sheet, leaving about 1 inch in between the cookies. Bake for 15 minutes. Cool on wire racks. Dust with powdered sugar and serve.

Pesca Infornata al Mosto Cotto e Amaretti

Baked Peaches with Cooked Must and Amaretti Cookies

A BIG PART of the flavor in this summertime dessert comes from the cooked *mosto* (in the form of Italian *vin cotto* or *saba*) that is used as an ingredient, as well as to finish the dish. Look for it in Italian grocery stores. For more about *vin cotto*, see page 38. Look for the largest fresh peaches in season for this recipe. If you can't find large-sized peaches, substitute smaller peaches, adjusting the recipe slightly if needed, and using two halves per serving instead of one.

SERVES 6

3 large peaches, white or yellow

1 tbsp unsweetened cocoa powder

1 tbsp powdered sugar

1 tbsp sambuca

1 tbsp cooked must (vin cotto or saba), plus as needed for garnish

2 large egg yolks

¼ tsp grated lemon zest

⅓ cup heavy cream

¾ cup crumbled amaretto cookies

3 cups ice cream, optional

1. Preheat the oven to 325°F.

2. Wash the peaches and cut them in half, removing the pit. Scoop out 1 tablespoon of the flesh from the center of each peach half, and set aside in a medium bowl to puree with the cocoa powder in step 3. Reserve the remaining peach halves separately.

3. Purée the peach flesh by hand or in a food processor with the cocoa powder, sugar, sambuca and the cooked must. Whisk in the egg yolks, lemon zest, and heavy cream; combine well. Slowly add the crumbled cookies. You should have a soft, but pliable, filling. Spoon the filling into the reserved peach halves. Place them in an ovenproof dish and bake at 325°F for about 20 minutes, until the filling is set. Remove from the oven and let cool slightly. Serve warm or at room temperature accompanied by a scoop of ice cream, if desired, and garnished with a bit of cooked must.

Salame di Cioccolato

Chocolate "Salami"

ANY DRY COOKIES could be used in this recipe; make sure they are not too greasy or too rich. Once you try this recipe, you'll want to start playing with it by trying out different ingredients. It is very easy to make and lots of fun when you serve it. Dried fruits, such as figs or apricots, added to the mixture are also good, just make sure the ingredients you add are not too dry. For a more adult version, you could add up to ⅓ cup of brandy, Amaretto, Strega, sambuca, or Grand Marnier for a good twist.

SERVES 4 TO 6

12 dry cookies (like vanilla or chocolate wafers) or 4 biscotti

¼ cup unsalted butter, soft but not melted

¼ cup finely chopped almonds or hazelnuts

⅓ cup semisweet chocolate chips

1 tbsp powdered sugar

1 large egg white, whisked until foamy

1. Break the cookies coarsely and set aside. Melt the chocolate gently in the microwave or in a double boiler over very low heat. Once melted, let it cool slightly.

2. In a bowl, whip the butter with the sugar until it is creamy. Add the almonds and the melted chocolate, and mix until well combined. Fold in the egg white, and then the cookies.

3. Line a loaf-style cake pan with waxed or parchment paper, and pour in the mixture. Cover with plastic wrap and place in refrigerator for 2 to 3 hours, or until completely set. Once set, remove it from the pan and slice as you would a traditional salami to serve.

Cannoli alla Siciliana

Sicilian Cannoli

CANNOLI RECIPES IN Sicily change from town to town, so just imagine how difficult is to find the "real" or original recipe, if one even exists. Well, this is a recipe I think works well. A friend of mine, Massimo Blanco, runs a little restaurant in Sicily, around the city of Palermo, where these cannoli are served daily. His secret is, without any doubt, the freshness of the ricotta, which is brought to him daily by a nearby farmer. Cow's milk ricotta may be substituted in this recipe, if you don't have access to sheep's milk ricotta. In any case, try to buy very fresh ricotta. If it looks grainy, pass it through a fine mesh sieve before making the filling. You will also need aluminum or stainless cannoli tubes for this recipe. You can find them in specialty shops or some Italian delis.

MAKES 20 CANNOLI

FOR THE CANNOLI DOUGH

2⅓ cups all-purpose flour

1 tbsp unsweetened cocoa powder

1 tbsp sugar

Pinch of salt

3 tbsp butter, melted

1 large egg white

1 tsp white vinegar

1 tbsp red wine or Marsala

FOR THE RICOTTA FILLING

1½ lb ricotta (smooth sheep's milk, if possible)

½ cup sugar

½ tsp vanilla extract

2 tbsp maraschino liqueur, optional

¾ cup small-dice candied fruit

¼ cup chopped blanched almonds or pistachios, shelled but not peeled

2 tbsp chopped dark chocolate

Tiny pinch of salt

1 cup all-purpose flour

1 egg white

4 cups vegetable oil, or as needed for frying

Powdered sugar, for dusting

1. *For the dough*: In a mixer with the paddle attachment, mix together all the dry ingredients. Slowly add the melted butter, egg white, vinegar, and the wine or Marsala. If the mixture is too dry to hold together, add a little bit of water. Once combined, remove, wrap in plastic wrap, and refrigerate for 1 hour.

2. *For the filling*: In a bowl, mix together the ricotta with the sugar, vanilla, liquor, if using, candied fruit, nuts, chocolate, and salt. Cover and refrigerate the filling until you are ready to fill the cannoli.

3. Preheat the oil in a deep fryer or a deep pot on the stove to 350°F.

4. Once you are ready to roll the cannoli, gather together 1 cup of flour for rolling, 1 egg

white beaten with a few drops of water as an eggwash, the cannoli tubes, and a pastry bag.

5. Roll out the dough by hand to a ¼-inch thickness and cut out 4-inch rounds or ovals.

6. Fold a round of dough around each tube, sealing the edges together with the egg white wash. (Make sure you don't touch the metal tubes with the egg wash.) Deep fry the "tubes" in hot oil until brown, about 2 to 3 minutes. Drain on paper towels, and let cool. When completely cooled, slip out the metal tubes.

7. Fill a pastry bag halfway with the ricotta filling and fill each pastry tube. Sprinkle with powdered sugar and serve.

CREMA COTTA MERINGATA E ABBRUSTOLITA

CREAM CUSTARD WITH BRULÉED MERINGUE

I HAD THIS dessert years ago in Umbria, on my way to Rome. I stopped at a wonderful restaurant which had this phenomenal interpretation of the classic French *crème brûlée*. I couldn't get the recipe at the time—the chef was very secretive about it—but after a few tries, I figured it out on my own.

SERVES 8

FOR THE CREAM CUSTARD

12 large egg yolks

⅔ cup sugar

¾ cup bitter cocoa powder, sifted

4 cups heavy cream

¼ tsp vanilla extract

FOR THE MERINGUE

3 large egg whites

1¾ cups powdered sugar, sifted

Zest of 1 lemon

FOR THE CHOCOLATE SAUCE

½ cup water

1 cup sugar

⅔ cup heavy cream

¾ cup unsweetened cocoa powder, sifted

1. *For the cream custard:* Preheat the oven to 300°F. Whip the yolks with the sugar until pale yellow and very thick, about 6 minutes. Add the cocoa powder and mix well. Add the cream and vanilla, strain it through a sieve, and let sit for about 20 minutes. Divide the mixture among 8 round or oval 3- to 4-ounce oven-proof ramekins. Place the ramekins in a roasting pan, and fill the pan with enough water to come halfway up the sides of the ramekins. Place the roasting pan on the middle rack in the oven and cook the custards in the water bath for about 1 hour, or until set. Let cool. Place in the refrigerator until very cold and ready to serve. *(recipe continues on next page)*

2. *For the meringue*: Preheat the oven to 425°F. Beat the egg whites while gradually adding the powdered sugar. Once you have medium peaks, add the lemon zest and continue beating until the egg whites are stiff. Use a piping bag to pipe the meringue over the previously prepared custards, and bake for 10 minutes, or just until the meringue is lightly browned.

3. *For the chocolate sauce*: In a small saucepan, combine the water with the sugar and bring to a boil. Add the cream and the cocoa powder. Let the mixture simmer over low heat, stirring occasionally, until the sauce is quite dense and thick, about 10 minutes. Strain the chocolate sauce through a fine mesh sieve and serve on the side with the custards.

BUDINO DI RISO CON FRAGOLINE DI BOSCO

RICE PUDDING WITH WILD STRAWBERRIES

THIS, IN A much simpler way, is a typical treat that mothers make when you are a child in Italy. You can make a savory version by omitting the egg yolks, berries, cream, sugar, and all the flavorings, and adding instead a small amount of salt, butter, and parmesan cheese to taste—simple and delicious.

SERVES 8

5 cups milk

¾ cup sugar

¾ cup Arborio rice

1 vanilla bean, scraped

5 large egg yolks

Zest of ½ lemon

½ cup heavy cream

3 pt wild strawberries

½ cup brown sugar, optional

1. In a medium saucepan, combine the milk, sugar, rice, vanilla bean (the seeds and the pod), and bring to a simmer over low heat. Once the milk mixture starts simmering, reduce the heat and stir, making sure the rice doesn't stick on bottom of pan, until rice is done, about 20 minutes or so. This should give you about 4½ cups of the rice mixture.

2. Remove from the heat and quickly stir in the yolks and lemon zest. Transfer the mixture to a bowl. Place the bowl in a larger bowl that has been partially filled with ice water. (Make sure the ice water level is low enough to keep it from splashing into the rice.) Stir the rice mixture over the ice water bath until cold. In a separate bowl, whip the cream. Remove the vanilla pod from the rice. Fold in the whipped cream in three additions.

3. Divide the pudding among 8 cups or ramekins (about ¾ cup of pudding in each). Place some berries on top of each serving, pressing them down slightly into the pudding. For a more sophisticated presentation, sprinkle some brown sugar on top and with a torch (or under a broiler or salamander) slightly burn the sugar until caramelized before placing the berries on top, and serve.

||||||||||||||||||

RECIPE NOTES

You may substitute ½ teaspoon of vanilla extract for the vanilla bean.

Try substituting other berries like blueberries, raspberries, or blackberries in place of the strawberries.

Crostata di Mandorle

Almond Tart

THIS RECIPE WILL make enough dough for two tarts; divide the dough into two pieces, wrap one and store it in the freezer, so there will be less work the next time you want to make this.

SERVES 8

FOR THE DOUGH

2⅓ cups all-purpose flour, sifted

⅓ cup sugar

½ tsp baking powder

Pinch of salt

Zest of 1 orange or lemon

¾ cup unsalted butter, cubed,
   cold (1½ sticks)

1 large egg

1 large egg yolk

1 tsp vanilla extract

1 tbsp heavy cream, as needed

FOR THE FILLING:

3 egg whites

1 cup sugar

2 cups chopped almonds

Zest of ½ lemon

1. *For the dough*: In a bowl or food processor, combine the flour, sugar, baking powder, salt, and zest. Add the cold butter cubes and toss lightly to coat. Pulse until the butter is the size of small peas. If you are doing this by hand, use a dough cutter and proceed in the same manner, making sure you don't heat the butter. In a separate bowl, combine the egg, egg yolk, vanilla, and heavy cream. Add it to the flour-butter mixture. Pulse (or mix quickly with your hands) until it begins to come together.

2. Turn the dough out onto a lightly floured surface and knead slightly. Do not overwork the dough. If it is too dry, add few drops of heavy cream. Divide the dough in half. Shape the halves into small disks and wrap individually in plastic wrap. Refrigerate one of the disks for at least 2 hours or overnight. (Place the other wrapped disc in a freezer-safe bag or air-

tight container and freeze for another use. The dough can be kept frozen for up to 2 months.)

3. Roll out one disk of the dough and press it into a tart pan (ideally, one with a removable bottom) that has been buttered and floured. Set aside. (If you aren't going to fill and bake the tart right away, wrap the dough with plastic wrap and keep it in the refrigerator. It will last for a day or two.)

4. *For the filling*: Preheat the oven to 325°F. Whip the egg whites, adding the sugar gradually after few minutes, until stiff, but shiny. Fold in the chopped almonds and the lemon zest. Pour into the prepared tart dough. If you wish, you may decorate the top of the tart with strips of additional dough.

5. Bake for about 30 minutes, or until a toothpick inserted in the center comes out dry. Remove and let cool.

Crostata del Trentino

Hazelnut Tart

THIS REMINDS ME of a wonderful tart that one of my relatives from Trentino (a region close to the Veneto where you can admire the most beautiful mountains) used to make, using her own hazelnuts from a tree in their backyard. She took the nuts out of the shell, toasted them, and then rolled them into flour using a bottle instead of a rolling pin. (She was frugal and never used the same rolling pin that she used for rolling fresh pasta—she said that the wood would get ruined from pressing on the nuts). In those days, there were no food processors, but if you have a food processor, it only takes a few minutes to put this together. Leave the skin on the nuts when you toast them.

SERVES 8

2½ cups all-purpose flour	1 egg yolk	¼ tsp cinnamon
¾ cup butter, softened	1 cup whole hazelnuts, whole, skin on	1 tsp rum
½ cup sugar	2 oz good-quality semi-sweet chocolate, melted and slightly cooled	1 cup raspberry jam or confiture
1 large egg		

1. In a food processor or by hand, combine all the ingredients, except the jam, and pulse or mix until the dough comes together. Do not overwork it. This will only take few seconds if you are using a food processor. Cover in plastic wrap and refrigerate for at least ½ hour.

2. Preheat the over to 350°F.

3. Roll or press ⅔ of the dough in a tart pan that has been buttered and floured, making sure you go up to the top, so it will hold the jam. Spread in the jam. Roll out the remaining dough into a circle about ⅛ inch thick. Cut it into strips and decorate the top of the tart. Make sure to crimp the edges of the dough strips to the bottom layer of dough along the rim of the pan. Bake for 30 to 35 minutes, or until the crust is a light golden color.

Colomba Pasquale

Easter Cake

THIS SWEET CAKE is typically served at the end of the meal on Easter Sunday. Each family buys this cake from their favorite local baker, as it can be a lot of effort to make. A true Easter cake is something between a brioche and a sweet bread, and normally requires lengthy preparation—three different risings—and you need to have the right oven for it to turn out properly. But this version is fast and easy, and nearly as good, so you'll probably make it more often. Serve with a warm, soft pastry cream mixed with a little heavy cream, or with a zabaglione or chocolate sauce, or even a good hazelnut or chocolate gelato.

SERVES 8

10 tbsp unsalted butter, cubed and
    softened

½ cup sugar

3 large eggs

2 cups cake four, sifted

1 tsp baking powder

Pinch of salt

Zest of 1 lemon

½ cup raisins, softened in rum or
    Marsala, squeezed of excess

¼ cup chopped tutti frutti or can-
    died fruit

1 tsp vanilla extract

¼ cup heavy cream or milk, warmed

1 large egg yolk, beaten (to brush
    the cake)

2 tbsp decorating sugar

½ cup chopped almonds, skin on

1. Preheat the over to 350°F.

2. Beat the butter with the sugar until very pale, about 6 minutes. Add the eggs, one at the time, beating after each addition. Slowly add in the flour, baking powder, salt, lemon zest (you may add some orange zest, too), raisins, tutti frutti, vanilla extract, and the cream or milk.

3. Grease an 8-inch cake pan (for an authentic *colomba pasquale*, use a molded cake pan shaped like a dove) with butter and coat with flour,

shaking out the excess. Spoon the batter into the cake pan—do not pour the batter out of the bowl, but actually spoon it into the pan. Brush the top with the egg yolk and sprinkle with some decorating sugar, and the almonds. Bake for 20 minutes. At this point, if the cake is starting to get too brown, cover it with aluminum foil, and finish cooking, another 12 to 15 minutes, or until a wooden toothpick inserted in the center comes out clean.

INDEX

ORIGINALLY FROM MAROSTICA, in Italy's Veneto region, Gianni Scappin holds a diploma from the Recoaro Terme Culinary Institute in Italy, and is a member of the Federation of Italian Chefs. Chef Scappin is a Certified Hospitality Educator (C.H.E.), and a lecturing instructor in culinary arts at The Culinary Institute of America, teaching in the kitchen of the Ristorante Caterina de' Medici, part of the college's Colavita Center for Italian Food and Wine. He is co-author of the cookbook *Cucina & Famiglia* (Morrow, 1999), and was consulting chef for the film *Big Night*. Chef Scappin was the owner and executive chef of Gigi Trattoria in Rhinebeck, New York, and executive chef at Le Madri, Moreno, and Castellano restaurants in New York City, as well as chef at restaurants in the Italian cities of Milan, Piedmonte, Montegrotto Terme, and Venice, and executive and corporate chef for the New York City-based Bice Group.

AN ASSISTANT PROFESSOR in Table Service at The Culinary Institute of America, Vincenzo Lauria is maître d' instructor in the Ristorante Caterina de' Medici at the CIA's Colavita Center for Italian Food and Wine. Mr. Lauria studied at the Istituto Professionale di Stato per Il Commerico Vittorio Veneto in Naples, Italy. He is a Certified Hospitality Educator (C.H.E.), a Certified Sommelier, and a member of the Sommelier Society of America. Prior to joining the CIA faculty, he held various restaurant ownership and management positions, including dining room manager of Aroma Osteria and general manager of Eddie's Gourmet Pizza in Wappingers Falls, New York, and wine captain and dining room director of Xavier's Restaurant Group in Garrison, New York.

A Note on the Type

This book was set in the OpenType Pro version of Adobe Jenson.
Like its typographic predecessors Centaur (Bruce Rogers, 1914) and
Arrighi (Frederic Warde, 1925), Jenson, the work of noted type designer
Robert Slimbach, looks back to the types of two esteemed Renaissance type
designers—the fifteenth-century Roman type of the French-born Venetian
printer Nicolas Jenson, sometimes credited as the "first true Roman," and the
sixteenth-century italic types cut by Ludovico degli Arrighi—as the basis for
this historical revival of their work. Originally released in 1996 as an Adobe
multiple master typeface, the OpenType Pro version adds the multi-
language support and typesetting refinements of that technology
to Slimbach's contemporary interpretation of the work
of two masters of Renaissance type design.

Art direction, design, and composition by Kevin Hanek

Printed in Malaysia